London Gateway

Maritime Archaeology in the Thames Estuary

By Antony Firth, Niall Callan, Graham Scott,
Toby Gane, and Stephanie Arnott

London Gateway

Maritime Archaeology in the Thames Estuary

By Antony Firth, Niall Callan, Graham Scott,
Toby Gane, and Stephanie Arnott

Illustrations by
Karen Nichols and Kitty Foster

Wessex Archaeology Report No. 30

Wessex Archaeology on behalf of DP World London Gateway 2012

British Library Cataloguing in Publication Data
A catalogue record for this book is available from the British Library

ISBN 978-1-874350-61-3

Published 2012 by Wessex Archaeology Ltd
Portway House, Old Sarum Park, Salisbury, SP4 6EB
Registered Charity in England and Wales, number 287786;
and in Scotland, Scottish Charity number SC042630
http://www.wessexarch.co.uk/

Edited by Alistair J. Barclay, Philippa Bradley and Julie Gardiner
Typeset and design by Karen Nichols
Cover design by Karen Nichols

Cover illustrations
Front: Schematic representation of ships and aircraft from the London Gateway scheme
Back: Multibeam image of Site 5056, the East Oaze Light Vessel

Printed by Henry Ling (Dorset Press) Ltd, Dorchester

Contents

List of Figures

List of Tables

Acknowledgements

The archaeological work was commissioned and funded by DP World London Gateway. Their support is greatly appreciated and in particular thanks go to David Lind, Marcus Pearson, Chris Webb, Tom Conroy, Katie Henry and Emma Deary.

Special thanks go to Gill Andrews, Consultant Archaeologist, who acted as the Archaeological Liaison Officer on behalf of DP World London Gateway, for her support and advice throughout the project.

Thanks go to the Port of London Authority for support and assistance in all aspects of fieldwork, in particular Peter Steen, Geoff Buckby, John Pinder, Alex Mortley, Nicola Clay and Kevin Leadbetter.

The curatorial input was provided by English Heritage (Ian Oxley, Peter Murphy and Chris Pater) and Essex County Council (Richard Havis). Thanks are due for their input into the project.

In addition, thanks go to Nick Shepherd (formerly at Oxford Archaeology) with his assistance during the EIA submission.

The project was managed on behalf of Wessex Archaeology by Stuart Leather, Dr Antony Firth and Toby Gane. Fieldwork and reporting was undertaken by Niall Callan, Graham Scott, Dietlind Paddenberg, Jens Auer, Brian Hession, Mark Beattie-Edwards, Kevin Stratford, Dan Pascoe, Stuart Churchley, Nicolas Bigourdan and Tom Burt. Acquisition and assessment of geophysical data was undertaken by Dr Paul Baggaley, Dr Louise Tizzard, Dr Stephanie Arnott and Patrick Dresch. Finds analysis was provided by Jacqueline McKinley, Lorraine Mepham and Graham Scott. In house finds conservation was provided by Lynn Wootten. Graphics and typesetting were undertaken by Karen Nichols and Kitty Foster. The publication was edited and managed by Dr Julie Gardiner, Dr Alistair Barclay and Philippa Bradley. The editors were assisted by Vic Cooper and Andrew Powell.

We are also grateful to Dr Joe Flatman for his advice and comments and to Alex Mortley, Chris Pater, Euan McNeill and Dr Paul Baggaley for kindly reading the text.

Thanks are due to the following organisations for allowing the reproduction of the following images: DP World – Figs 8 (dredger) and 54 (London Gateway port); National Maritime Museum – Fig. 20, (the *London*, ref. PX6182), Fig. 22 (Thames bawleys, ref. G03605), Fig. 35 (*Dynamo*, ref. P16465), Fig. 40 (SS *Letchworth*, ref. B0891/36), and Fig. 49 (*Wilna*, ref. F9305); Thames Discovery Programme – Fig. 25 (cannon); State Library of Victoria – Fig. 32 (*Dovenby* ref. H99.220/4483); National Archives – Fig. 45 (Anti-submarine boom); Lancashire County Library and Information Service – Fig. 47 (*Phyllis Rosalie*). All other images are copyright Wessex Archaeology.

Abbreviations and Conventions

ALSF	Aggregate Levy Sustainability Fund
AMF	Archaeological Mitigation Framework
BULSI	Build-Use-Loss-Survival-Investigation
CMS	Clearance Mitigation Statement
DCMS	Department of Culture Media and Sport
DEMS	Defensively Equipped Merchant Ship
dGPS	Differential Global Positioning System
EIA	Environmental Impact Assessment
ES	Environmental Statement
GIS	Geographic information system
HEEP	Historic Environment Enabling Programme
HEO	Harbour Empowerment Order
JCCC	Joint Casualty and Compassionate Centre
MALSF	Marine Aggregate Levy Sustainability Fund
MoU	Memoranda of Understanding
MSA	*Merchant Shipping Act*
NGO	Non-governmental organization
NMR/NRHE	National Monuments Record
OPA	Outline Planning Application
PLA	Port of London Authority
PMRA	*Protection of Military Remains Act*
PWA	*Protection of Wrecks Act*
REC	Regional Environmental Characterisation
ROV	Remote operated vehicle
SCUBA	Self-contained underwater breathing apparatus
SoCG	Statements of Common Ground
SMR	Sites and Monuments Record
SR1	Sea Reach 1 (navigational buoy)
TDP	Thames Discovery Programme
TWA	Tidal Works Approval
TWAO	Transport and Works Act Order
UKHO	UK Hydrographic Office
USBL	Ultra Short Baseline (or SSBL – Super Short Baseline)
WSI	Written Scheme of Investigation

Foreword

Simon Moore – CEO DP World

It is often said that geography is one of the main reasons for the success of London as a city. Proximity to the open sea, via a fast flowing, tidal river such as the Thames was always going to be an attractive proposition for people looking to trade. From the early Roman founders of *Londinium* to their modern day equivalents, the UK capital has an ancient history of trade, movement of goods and people.

The area on which we are developing the new port of London Gateway is one of significant natural and archaeological interest. Developing such a vast, modern port facility in such a sensitive location has brought numerous challenges. As an organisation, we are acutely aware that we have environmental responsibilities and we take them extremely seriously.

We are committed to safeguarding habitats and to ensuring that the histories of communities living in the Thames Estuary are respected and remembered. Archaeological investigation ahead of marine dredging has made a significant contribution both to our understanding of the history of the estuary and to the development of investigative methods and approaches. London Gateway has been at the forefront of marine development-led archaeology on major infrastructure projects for the last decade and this volume presents the key issues which have emerged.

Marcus Pearson BSc – Environmental Manager

From the outset it was recognized that construction of London Gateway would have implications for the historic marine environment. A substantial programme of dredging in the navigable channel was required to allow access for the next generation of the world's largest container ships; it was known that there were a number of potential historic wreck sites along this channel which would have to be cleared before dredging could take place.

In anticipation of these works an extensive programme of marine archaeological work was undertaken by Wessex Archaeology to ensure that historic remains were identified, studied and where appropriate, protected. This programme accompanied the largest ever post-war navigational clearance operation in the Thames, carried out on behalf of London Gateway by the Port of London Authority. A number of locations were considered so significant that the design of the channel was amended to enable their preservation *in situ*.

The works have provided an important opportunity to rethink the intellectual and methodological approaches to maritime infrastructure archaeology. This project and its findings have had a significant effect on what we know about the historic environment of the Thames and on the way in which maritime archaeology is conducted in connection with major infrastructure schemes. The result is this volume – *Maritime Archaeology in the Thames Estuary*. It has implications which extend beyond the Thames Estuary and its publication is intended to inform and stimulate all those concerned with delivering sustainable marine development within the context of the historic environment.

Throughout the programme we have benefited from discussions with the Port of London Authority, English Heritage and Essex County Council. The project's success has been due to the integrated approach which was adopted for the work; archaeologists, dredging contractors, developers and regulators have all worked effectively together with enthusiasm and commitment.

The archaeological discoveries will be made available to a wider public both through the deposition of the finds and site archive with Southend Museum, Essex, and through the newly opened Thurrock Thameside Visitor Centre. It is intended that the Centre will form a focal point for local residents and visitors, enhancing their enjoyment of the area and their awareness of its rich environment and heritage.

Introduction

London Gateway. Maritime Archaeology in the Thames Estuary is intended to inform and stimulate all those who have an interest in the maritime archaeology of the Thames or are concerned with achieving marine development that is sustainable with respect to the historic environment.

London Gateway (properly DP World London Gateway, hereafter London Gateway) is a major development of an entirely new container terminal built on a largely brownfield site on the north bank of the Thames near Stanford-le-Hope (Figs 1, 2) (Biddulph *et al.* 2012). Construction of the terminal has been accompanied by a capital dredging scheme to increase the depth of the navigable channel to the new port. In the outer reaches of the Thames, the depth is naturally greater than required for navigation so dredging has been limited to some relatively small sections. Further upstream, however, where the Thames narrows into the Yantlet Channel, very extensive dredging has been required.

Over the course of a decade, a series of marine archaeological investigations has taken place that provides a new perspective on the historic environment of the Thames and the conduct of maritime archaeology. This volume seeks to encapsulate and draw together the methodological and intellectual process as well as the archaeological results, starting with the evolution of the project, its context and constraints, because of the strong role these factors played in deciding the methods to be used and the sites that would be examined.

This experience merits publication because it is relevant to understanding the emergence and trajectory of marine development-led archaeology in the UK in three respects. First, London Gateway has influenced the way in which maritime archaeology is conducted in connection with major infrastructure schemes. Second, it has had a practical effect on the methodologies employed in maritime archaeology. Third, the project has changed what we know and regard as important about the historic environment of the Thames. These three strands have been used to organise the book: Part I sets out the investigative framework through which archaeological work was integrated with the assessment and preparation of a major marine development; Part II describes the desk-based, geophysical and diver-based methodologies that were used; and Part III presents a thematic account of the sites that were investigated. The final section – Discussion: A New Maritime Archaeology of the Thames Estuary? – considers innovations and outcomes with the intention of providing both critical and positive support for the on-going development of maritime archaeology in connection with major infrastructure projects both in the UK and further afield.

The investigations reported in this volume started over a decade ago, when maritime archaeology in the UK was at a different stage. London Gateway has both accommodated and helped shape changes that encompass techniques and technologies, new knowledge about the composition and importance of the marine historic environment, and the introduction of new legal and policy frameworks. In this, the role of London Gateway as a conscientious developer must be underlined; as will become clear below, the developer's actions with respect to maritime archaeology were not dictated. Rather, the Thames Estuary provided a fluid and not always comfortable space within which London Gateway played its part in fostering development-led archaeology at sea. London Gateway commitment to best practice is such that this volume incorporates archaeological investigations initiated and managed by the Port of London Authority (PLA) as well as investigations for which London Gateway and its predecessor P&O were directly responsible.

London Gateway is not the first or only major infrastructure project that has involved marine archaeology, either in the UK or around the world. Nor did it take place within a bubble, impervious to the experience of major infrastructure projects on land or other forms of archaeological investigation at sea. As indicated above, London Gateway took place within a dynamic context, but it also had an influence on its context that we hope to illustrate here. We do not, however, provide a global or even UK-wide review of progress in maritime archaeological frameworks, approaches and techniques; rather, we present a record of our own experience, both positive and negative, in the expectation that there are contributions here that will prove useful to others.

The interplay between London Gateway and other projects during a very dynamic period for UK marine archaeology was significant. Marine archaeology was a focus of major funding through the Aggregate Levy Sustainability Fund (ALSF), administered by English Heritage, from 2002 to 2011, which prompted and supported a tremendous range of projects that addressed questions of methodology, baseline data and management approaches (Flatman and Doeser 2010). London Gateway certainly drew upon some of the advances being made, but it also helped to frame the thinking that gave rise to some ALSF projects – notably *Wrecks on the Seabed*, *On the Importance of Shipwrecks*, and *Assessing Boats and Ships* (Hamel 2011; Wessex Archaeology 2006a; 2011a–d). There was also mutual learning in the course of methodological developments under the Contract for the Provision of Archaeological Services in Support of the *Protection of Wrecks Act* 1973, for which Wessex Archaeology was responsible from 2003 onwards. The mutual relevance increased significantly when the 17th-century warship *London* (see below) was designated under the 1973 Act

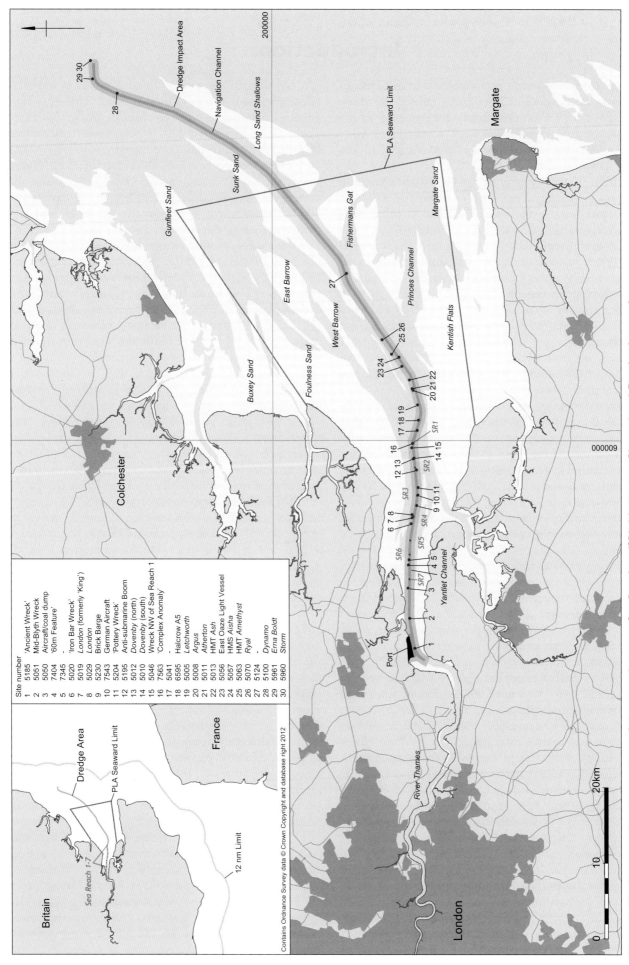

Site number	
1	5185	'Ancient Wreck'
2	5051	Mid-Blyth Wreck
3	5050	Aircraft/coal dump
4	7404	'60m Feature'
5	7345	–
6	5020	'Iron Bar Wreck'
7	5019	*London* (formerly 'King')
8	5029	*London*
9	5230	Brick Barge
10	7543	German Aircraft
11	5204	'Pottery Wreck'
12	5195	Anti-submarine Boom
13	5012	*Dovenby* (north)
14	5010	*Dovenby* (south)
15	5046	Wreck NW of Sea Reach 1
16	7563	'Complex Anomaly'
17	5041	–
18	6595	Halcrow A5
19	5005	*Letchworth*
20	5008	*Argus*
21	5011	*Atherton*
22	5013	HMT *Ash*
23	5056	East Oaze Light Vessel
24	5057	HMS *Aisha*
25	5063	HMT *Amethyst*
26	5070	*Ryal*
27	5124	–
28	5100	*Dynamo*
29	5961	*Erna Boldt*
30	5960	*Storm*

Contains Ordnance Survey data © Crown Copyright and database right 2012

Figure 1: Site location showing position of sites in relation to Sea Reaches (SR), Navigation Channel and Dredge Impact Area

in 2008. London Gateway was also one amongst many development-led schemes at this time, and although it had a magnitude and complexity that set it apart, many of the concerns examined in this volume were also being discussed in the context of other schemes; the investigation of sites such as the 16th-century Gresham Ship (Auer and Firth 2007) and the 17th-century Swash Channel Wreck (Wessex Archaeology 2006b) both had particular resonance with London Gateway.

The term 'maritime' archaeology has been used intentionally in the subtitle of the volume and the introductory text above because this volume is concerned primarily with the human past as understood and appreciated through the physical remains of ships, boats and associated infrastructure. The specific investigations reported here were concerned with remains found underwater in the sea, so the terms 'marine' or 'underwater' archaeology might be used, but these terms encompass the investigation of remains of other aspects of the human past that can be found in or near the sea or other bodies of water. There is no consideration here of prehistoric sites once on land but now submerged, or of the wide range of coastal activity sites found around the Thames. Nor do we address maritime sites that were once wet but now form land, as a result of very substantial reclamation of the margins of the Thames in the past. This is not to say that we were blind to these other aspects of archaeology. Marine studies in the course of the Environmental Impact Assessment (EIA) demonstrated the presence of features of prehistoric interest, and of coastal interest in intertidal areas. However, in the case of prehistoric deposits their position generally at levels below the depth of planned dredging, and their greater accessibility via a land-based approach to deposit modelling, meant that submerged prehistory did not form a significant strand of the activities reported here. Similarly, the history of reclamation has meant that the most important traces of previous coastal activity have been identified on former coastlines well within the dryside of the scheme, and are reported in an accompanying volume (Biddulph *et al.* 2012).

This volume details the start of maritime archaeology in connection with London Gateway in the knowledge that investigations are still on-going. Specifically, the construction phase – involving one of the largest capital dredging schemes ever conducted in the UK – has been accompanied by a series of archaeological measures that were still being applied and developed whilst this volume was in preparation. The construction phase investigations, and their implications for reconsidering the effectiveness of all that is reported here, will be published in due course.

As noted above, the London Gateway investigations took place at a time when maritime archaeology in the UK was at a different stage. It is in the character of development that approaches adopted early in the process become formalised in the documentation that is agreed with regulators. London Gateway, in common with other major infrastructure schemes, adopted an

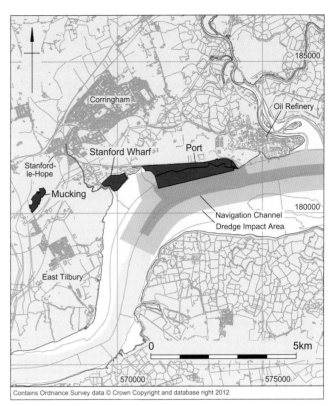

Figure 2: Location of the London Gateway Port in relation to Stanford Wharf and Mucking

inherently flexible form of documentation that could adapt to new data coming to light. Nonetheless it must be recognised that some of the archaeological approaches and decisions are already 'of their time' even though the investigations described here are relatively recent. The decisions accompanying maritime archaeology in connection with development-led schemes today are already different to those of London Gateway, reflecting in part the formative role that this scheme has had.

This is the first extensive account of maritime archaeology in the Thames to be based directly upon physical archaeological remains from the bed of the estuary itself, rather than from its margins, hinterland or upper reaches. The proposed dredging provided a 400m wide transect along the length of the estuary covering a distance of 100km from London Gateway Port to 25km off Harwich (Fig. 1). The transect is not continuous, as the dredging proposed in the outer estuary only covered specific sections where the natural depth was insufficient. These shorter sections added to a largely continuous 27km strip of proposed dredging in the Yantlet Channel in the inner estuary. This was a very extensive archaeological project by any measure, comparable to major terrestrial linear projects such as road schemes (eg M6 Toll (Powell *et al.* 2008); A120 (Timby *et al.* 2007) and rail links (eg High Speed 1 (see for example, Booth *et al.* 2011)). As major linear schemes and other large-scale terrestrial developments (major new housing developments, gravel quarries and airports: Bradley *et al.* 2011) changed the understanding of the UK historic environment by presenting arbitrary samples of the archaeological composition of the countryside, so too does London Gateway change what we know, and think is important, about maritime archaeology in the estuary.

In 1999, *An Archaeological Research Framework for the Greater Thames Estuary* (Williams and Brown 1999) made the following observation:

> 'It seems reasonable to assume that shipwreck has been a constant factor throughout this long history of sea and water-borne activity. Navigational hazards abound in the river and estuary, and wartime losses have also occurred. It is evident that the study area potentially contains important archaeological evidence associated with key aspects of Britain's development as a maritime nation and world power'

This Research Framework also noted that:
> 'The current archaeological record ... is dominated by the remains of relatively modern craft with very little evidence available for vessels from the medieval and early post-medieval periods'.

There was, however, no acknowledgement that the archaeological record was essentially a transcription of navigational hazards; at the start of the London Gateway project, very little of this 'archaeological record' had received any form of archaeological scrutiny.

This volume outlines how one transect of the archaeological record of the Thames has been scrutinised. In one sense, it simply confirms Williams and Brown's (1999) observation that evidence for vessels from the medieval and early post-medieval periods are still elusive. One consequence is that we do not provide an overarching chronological narrative of the maritime archaeology of the Thames; the earliest finds reported here are post-medieval. The maritime history of the Thames is, of course, much older and encompasses evidence found on land, in intertidal areas and underwater that stretches back deep into prehistory. Even setting aside the evidence of landing sites and wharves, of artefacts that must have travelled by sea, of iconography and document, the Thames has an impressive legacy of discoveries of early ships and boats

(Milne 1985; 2003; Marsden 1996). In line with the Research Framework, modern craft are dominant here. London Gateway has, however, created the need to contemplate these modern craft with much greater differentiation, because the project has found and recognised smaller wooden-hulled vessels likely to have been used for fishing and trading as well as the metal-hulled cargo ships most often identified in hydrographic records. In addition, as anticipated by the Research Framework, wartime losses are a key component of the maritime archaeology of the estuary. But again, London Gateway demands greater differentiation. As shown below, the wartime wrecks are monuments to extraordinary times, when shipping was both fundamental to the whole country's survival and involved in desperate events. Even where there is no recorded loss of life, these wrecks are an important reminder of experiences that today's generations might find difficult to imagine. London Gateway also shows that the wartime losses are not an undifferentiated mass; each loss ought to be considered in its own terms and context, linked to different events, campaigns and themes. In the same way that road scheme archaeology drew attention away from large-scale sites, grandiose castles and villas, to settlements and their wider landscape context, London Gateway has largely dealt with ships and boats that had no claim to fame other than to the communities who built, used and were lost with them.

London Gateway has contributed to the maritime archaeology of the Thames Estuary at a time when maritime archaeology across the UK was in major flux. In terms of marine development-led archaeology for major infrastructure projects, new technologies and methodologies, and new understanding and appreciation of the marine historic environment, London Gateway was at or near the front for a decade. Many of the changes in methodologies and technologies occurred as a result of separate pressures, but London Gateway is important to understanding the direction that maritime archaeology is taking in the UK and perhaps more widely. The following narrative illustrates why we think this to be so.

Part I
Investigative Framework

LONDON GATEWAY AND THE HISTORIC ENVIRONMENT OF THE THAMES

Wessex Archaeology's first involvement in the London Gateway project was in 2001, in the early stages of developing the Environmental Impact Assessment (EIA) to accompany the application for consent to build the new port. The scheme had been initiated by P&O who, in 2006, were purchased by DP World.

In developing the EIA, P&O were assisted by consultants Royal Haskoning for the marine elements (known as 'wetside') and Oscar Faber for the land-based elements ('dryside'). Archaeological aspects of the EIA were also split: Oxford Archaeology was appointed to address the dryside, and Wessex Archaeology to handle the wetside. Gill Andrews was appointed as Archaeological Liaison Officer (ALO) to oversee and co-ordinate the archaeological programmes to achieve an integrated approach. To this end, all of the archaeological elements of the EIA – both wetside and dryside – fell within Oscar Faber's remit.

In the course of developing the EIA, the role of archaeological curator for the wetside largely fell to English Heritage, with Essex County Council taking the lead on the dryside. Kent County Council was responsible for curatorial input for dryside elements of the scheme on the southern (Kent) bank of the Thames. The responsibilities of these authorities, and others, are discussed at greater length below.

Following submission of the EIA in 2002–3, archaeological attention on the wetside switched to the enabling works that would need to be carried out before dredging could take place. In particular, it was known that there was a series of wrecks and obstructions along the navigable channel, some of which were quite large, which would have to be cleared before dredging could take place. The pre-dredge clearance of these wrecks and obstructions was to be carried out by the Port of London Authority (PLA). The PLA is the local statutory authority responsible for maintaining the navigation of the Thames. Under section 120 of the *Port of London Act* 1968, the PLA has a legal obligation to remove or otherwise destroy sunken wrecks if they are likely to interfere with navigation. However, under section 48A of the *Harbours Act* 1964, the powers of port authorities such as the PLA are subject to a duty to maintain access to features of archaeological interest. This duty, combined with a wish to develop best practice in the light of the PLA's then recent experience of the 16th-century 'Gresham Ship' found in the Princes Channel (Auer and Firth 2007) (Figs 3–4), led to the PLA commissioning Wessex Archaeology to assist with archaeological aspects of the anticipated wreck clearance programme.

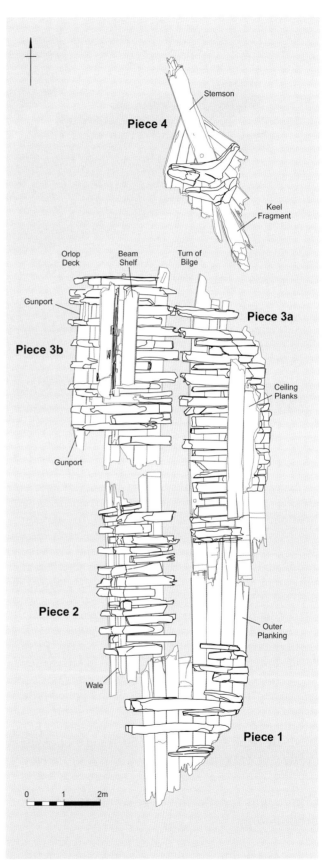

Figure 3: The Gresham Ship: plan of the surviving hull fragments on the seabed

6

London Gateway. Maritime Archaeology in the Thames Estuary

Figure 4: Raising of the Gresham Ship

Archaeological investigations in advance of clearance provide the majority of the results reported here. Existing data were reviewed in order to develop a framework for mitigating the impact of clearance, and then a series of desk-based, geophysical and diver-based investigations took place in order to prepare Clearance Mitigation Statements (CMS) (see Part III, below) for each of the wrecks/obstructions of archaeological interest that might be impacted by clearance.

The final CMSs were completed in 2008, by which time London Gateway had received its consent. By then detailed preparations were being made for construction to commence. Small-scale clearance activities were carried out by the PLA throughout the period. Major clearance activities took place in 2010 with on-site recording by the Thames Discovery Programme (TDP). Dredging commenced in March 2010 and is on-going at the time of writing.

Challenges for marine development-led archaeology

One reason for detailing the place of maritime archaeology within the London Gateway scheme is the relative paucity of available literature on marine development-led archaeology. The grey literature of client reports, EIA documents and supporting appendices is expanding rapidly, containing all sorts of detail of the marine historic environment, but grey literature does not generally concern itself with how the projects themselves have developed, the problems encountered, or the lessons learned. The account here, therefore, is intended to set the experience of London Gateway alongside publications on other marine development-led projects such as the Slufter project in the Netherlands (Adams *et al.* 1990), the Storebaelt in Denmark (Pedersen *et al.* 1997), the Immersed Tunnel Project in Oslo (Gundersen 2010) and Ormen Lange Pipeline on the Norwegian Continental Shelf (Bryn *et al.* 2007). A specific literature on this particular aspect of marine archaeology is important because it is already the case in the UK that the majority of marine archaeological investigations are being prompted either by marine development schemes, or by more generalised plans for marine development for which archaeological strategies are required. In this respect, marine archaeology is following the path of development-led archaeology on land in the UK through the 1980s and 1990s. As the references above show, development is already a major driver for marine archaeological investigations in other parts of the world and seems likely to become an increasingly important influence on the discipline globally. Outcomes will be better if experience is shared.

Previously in the UK, marine archaeological investigations have occurred either as a consequence of the efforts of individual researchers examining particular places or shipwrecks around which small teams have been built; or as a reaction to the unexpected discovery of an interesting site or wreck, again prompting the development of a team to carry out investigations. Such teams have generally had to rely on their own resources or draw upon piecemeal funding. With a few exceptions, there has been relatively little systematic funding from public authorities. Before 2002, public funding for marine investigations had been spread thinly across numerous and geographically disparate sites in connection with statutory responsibilities, notably in support of the *Protection of Wrecks Act* 1973, or had comprised modest but welcome support for site-specific initiatives and for efforts to engage recreational divers and the wider public.

Marine archaeological investigations prompted by development are quite different. The focus of interest is usually an area rather than a site, and it is chosen by the developer not the archaeologist. It is often the case, moreover, that the development site is in a difficult environment for conducting archaeological investigations. The infrastructure and technological capabilities that can be brought to bear are considerable and are applied far more extensively than has usually been the case for site-specific investigations. Whilst funding is made available by the developer, it is provided to meet their overall objectives (securing or satisfying consent) rather than achieving archaeological outcomes as such, and the relationship is one of client and contractor in which value for money, tested competitively, is a key factor. As on land, development-led archaeology at sea has led to the establishment of 'standing' teams of archaeologists able to develop specialised skills that can be deployed from project to project, together with the necessary technical and business support, independent of public authorities and not as susceptible, therefore, to the sudden end of resources when an individual project comes to an end.

Although bringing advantages, marine development-led archaeology also brings definite challenges, especially when the scheme is on the scale of London Gateway and in an environment that is both difficult and historically-rich, like the Thames. In the course of work, considerable effort was directed to questions which will be common to other development-led schemes, for which we hope our own experiences will provide some assistance in future. These questions encompass:

• The difficulties of dealing with the environment;
• Uncertainty about what archaeological material might be present;
• The cost of investigations;
• And the possible importance of the sites in archaeological terms.

Environment

The Thames is a difficult place to carry out archaeological work, both from the surface and underwater. Underwater visibility is very poor – often zero, rarely as much as a couple of metres. The estuary has a moderate tidal range (5.3m at Southend on High Water Springs, Admiralty Chart 1185), causing tidal currents such that it is only possible to dive during 'slack' periods of an hour or so at each high water and low water. The tidal currents also cause difficulty to survey vessels, which generally can work only up and down the tide rather than across. Anchoring of vessels is also severely hampered by the tides, especially if the weather is unfavourable. Whilst the eastward-facing Thames might appear to be reasonably sheltered in the lee of prevailing westerly winds, it is quite wide throughout the sections where work has taken place – 2km at London Gateway Port; 7km off Southend; >30km at Sea Reach 1 (SR 1) – providing sufficient fetch for wind and swell to build. In the outer estuary, the Thames is effectively open sea. Further, the Thames can also act as a funnel, concentrating and increasing tidal surges caused by weather in the North Sea, as experienced during fieldwork in November 2007.

The Thames is a major thoroughfare for large ships, placing a further constraint on surveying and diving operations. In particular, constant use of the estuary meant that it was not possible to deploy fixed infrastructure, such as temporary moorings or survey beacons. Finally, the Thames is extensive and not over-endowed with small ports suitable for smaller vessels, meaning that quite a lot of time was taken up 'in transit' from base to work place.

Mastering these environmental difficulties in a cost-effective manner has been a common question for London Gateway, always keeping in mind the risks to personnel but conscious too of the risks to the success of an investigation from weather or equipment failure.

Uncertainty

Coping with uncertainty was a second major question for both archaeologists and developers.

Because of its environment, its long history of maritime activity, and its importance in a series of conflicts, many boats and ships have come to grief in the Thames. The environment has also rendered the Thames inscrutable for the majority of this history, so knowledge of what lies beneath its waters was lacking, certainly at the start of the investigations described here. Even where wrecks are known to be present, their identity and age were often unknown.

Not only was there uncertainty about what might have sunk beneath the Thames, there was uncertainty too about what might have survived the complex natural and cultural processes that have affected the bed of the estuary; about what might be visible to archaeological instruments; and about what the traces shown by such instruments might actually mean in terms of features on the seabed.

There was further uncertainty about the balances to be struck between knowledge and risk in the development process, ranging from what might constitute an acceptable EIA to what risk might be posed to the dredging programme by a hitherto unidentified site suddenly coming to light.

Cost

Closely linked to the difficulties of the environment and uncertainty was the question of cost, both in absolute terms and in relation to the stage of works. In particular, costs incurred prior to consent being granted would be 'at risk' if the scheme were to be turned down, hence a preference for investigations to be deferred until consent was assured. The refusal of the Dibden Terminal port scheme in 2004, following an estimated £45 million expended in EIA studies, underlined this potential risk (internet source: Maritime Journal). Even after consent for London Gateway was granted, the amount of investment required for such a major scheme in advance of any financial return introduced another pressure to defer investigations until construction was assured. However, as the most obvious means of reducing risks is to increase knowledge through further investigations, deferring costs to a later stage could actually risk the investment made so far if the level of knowledge was held unsatisfactory.

Of particular concern was whether expenditure would be incurred but to negligible effect, wasted by poor weather or by achieving results that were inconclusive. Environmental and logistical constraints required high-cost solutions, but with windows for fieldwork so very limited, the risk that valuable resources could not be deployed effectively was a major concern.

Importance

The balance between costs, uncertainty and environment was manifest in questions about archaeological importance. Neither the environment nor funding would allow unlimited access to the historic environment, either to understand its presence and character, or to establish how best to mitigate the anticipated impacts. Archaeological approaches would have to be selective, involving clear choices to direct attention and resources to some features but not others. Such choices were to be based on what was thought to be most archaeologically important, on several levels.

Within the maritime sphere, debate has focused on the relative importance of sites which are known and sites which are merely suspected on the basis of ambiguous geophysical traces. As the possible sites indicated only by geophysical traces are relatively ephemeral, and given the PLA's concern for clearing items that might impede dredging, then it was the confirmed sites that received most attention. The approaches to this complex question are discussed at greater length below.

Even amongst the 'known' sites, questions of importance persisted. Some sites were clearly important or likely to be so – such as the 17th-century warship *London* (Site 5019/5029) and the 'Iron Bar Wreck' (Site 5020) – but as discussed below these sites were avoided by dredging, so their investigation for the purposes of the scheme was less necessary. Other sites, whilst known and within the dredging area, were of uncertain character and might prove to be inconsequential debris or dumps of material. A further class of sites were relatively well-known but dated predominantly to the 20th century, so their importance was initially considered to be more historical or social than archaeological. All of these points were contentious, and contended, in the course of the project's development.

THE LEGAL, PLANNING AND CURATORIAL FRAMEWORK

Several public authorities have legal responsibilities encompassing the London Gateway scheme. The dryside is predominantly on land within the county of Essex, but some proposed reclamation for the new port and quay extended across intertidal areas and out into the fully tidal areas of the Thames. In general terms, county boundaries stop at low water mark; they do not extend into fully sub-tidal areas. As well as delimiting the counties, these boundaries also provide the principal means of demarcating the legal extent of 'England'. Hence in general terms 'England', made up of the counties, also stops at low water. In a few cases, including major indentations in the coast caused by estuaries like the Thames, the county boundary is drawn straight across the estuary (Fig. 5), incorporating areas below low water mark within the county, and therefore within 'England'.

The county boundaries of Essex and Kent extend straight across the Thames from Southend on the north bank to the Isle of Grain on the south, downstream of the new port, with the upstream part of the estuary split equally between the two counties by a dividing line along the middle of the estuary. Consequently, the dryside part of the new port, including its reclaimed areas and quay, lay wholly within Essex, while the channel where dredging was to take place is split between Essex and Kent as far as Southend/Isle of Grain; downstream of this point the channel is outside the county boundaries.

There is a further complexity; whilst the county boundaries of Kent and Essex extend over the sub-tidal channel, their boundaries as planning authorities may remain limited to low water. This is important because the system of planning law administered through local authorities is central to the conduct of development-led archaeology on land in the UK. In planning law, archaeology is a 'material consideration' in deciding whether a development can go ahead, including what archaeological information needs to be made available for decision-making, and what conditions might accompany consent. At the time London Gateway was

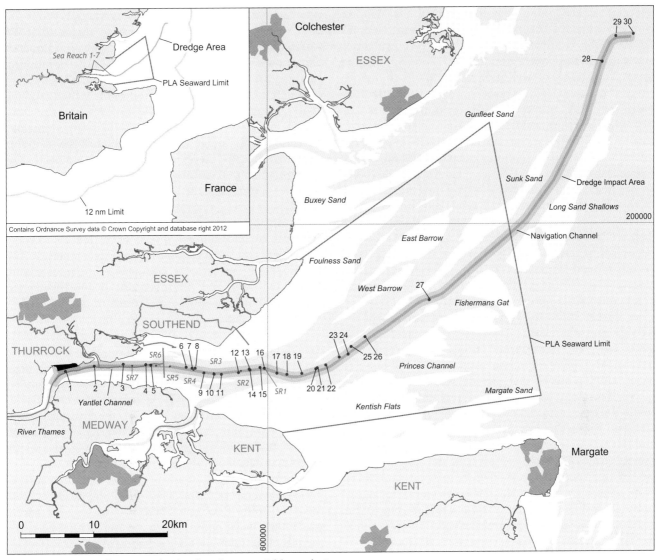

Figure 5: Sites in relation to the legal and curatorial boundaries

being considered, this basic mechanism was codified in *Planning Policy Guidance 16: Archaeology and Planning* (Department of the Environment 1990, superseded at the time of writing by the *National Planning Policy Framework*) and included archaeological principles that also applied the other forms of consent required by major infrastructure projects. The ambiguity over boundaries meant that, even though bits of the tidal Thames might be within a county, they were not necessarily subject to the planning law that the county administered.

The relevance of the county boundaries to the definition of England is also important because, at the time archaeological activities at London Gateway got underway, the statutory remit of English Heritage was limited to 'England'. This was not changed until the passing of the *National Heritage Act* 2002, which extended English Heritage's remit to territorial waters (ie to waters up to 12 miles beyond England). As English Heritage had no remit beyond England at the start of the project, it had no specialist staff, corpus of practice or comprehensive policy with respect to marine archaeology, except that the National Monuments

Record (NMR), now the National Record of the Historic Environment (NRHE), included data relating to wrecks and casualties in territorial waters.

As a consequence, there was a very real gap in curatorial provision for the wetside of London Gateway at the outset of the project. Even though, technically, wetside elements of the scheme upstream of Southend/Isle of Grain were within England, the general restriction of English Heritage's remit to low water meant that it had little practical capability. Equally, although these same areas were within Essex and Kent, there was a question mark over whether they lay within the scope of the planning authorities, through which curatorial advice was provided. Moreover, all areas of the wetside downstream of Southend/Isle of Grain were, until 2002, unambiguously beyond the remit of either national or local archaeological curators.

Other authorities had a role in the wetside, both upstream and downstream of Southend/Isle of Grain. Of these, the most significant has been the PLA, whose area extends from far upstream at Teddington down to a series of straight lines across the estuary – from Foulness, out to sea, across the estuary, and back to

Sheppey – recognising that the channel for London Gateway extended beyond the PLA boundary to a point off Harwich. As noted above, the PLA's responsibilities are set out in the *Port of London Act* 1968 and, include maintaining safety of navigation using powers to remove wreck if necessary. These powers provided the statutory basis for PLA to carry out preparatory work for clearance, and the clearance work itself. In support of its legal responsibilities, the PLA maintains a range of operational services, including hydrographic survey vessels, salvage teams and divers, all of which fed into the archaeological work. Archaeological input was provided by the PLA through its River Regime and Environment Manager. The PLA is also a regulatory authority on the Thames by virtue of the *Port of London Act* 1968, hence construction of the port and the dredging itself required Tidal Works Approval and the PLA became closely involved in establishing and monitoring the conditions placed on the development.

A further authority with key powers throughout the wetside is the Receiver of Wreck within the Maritime and Coastguard Agency, by virtue of powers set out in the *Merchant Shipping Act* (MSA) 1995. The MSA 1995 requires that anyone who finds or takes possession of any wreck in UK waters must give notice to the Receiver, who will administer the provisions of the Act with respect to original owners, awards to salvors, and ownership of unclaimed wreck. The powers of the Receiver of Wreck overlap with the powers of the PLA with respect to wreck. In order to avoid duplication and confusion, it was agreed that wreck of archaeological interest would be administered under the MSA 1995, whereas wreck of no archaeological interest would be administered under Section 120 of the *Port of London Act.*

Under the *Protection of Military Remains Act* (PMRA) 1986, all crashed military aircraft are 'protected places', protected against unauthorised interference. The PMRA is administered by the Joint Casualty and Compassionate Centre (JCCC) of the Ministry of Defence (MoD). This Act also provides that sunk and stranded vessels can be protected by designation, either as 'protected places' or as 'controlled sites'. The MoD's view in 2001 was that the definition of vessels in military service only included military vessels, not merchant vessels being used for military purposes. Even with this narrow definition, there were several small warships known in the wetside area that were eligible for designation, though there were no designations in force. The definition of 'vessels in military service' was tested through the courts in 2005–6 with the result that a broader definition, including merchant vessels in certain circumstances, started to apply. Although there were no designations in the Thames, there were several wrecks that might be eligible for designation under this broader definition.

The other main form of wreck designation relevant to London Gateway was the *Protection of Wrecks Act* (PWA) 1973, administered directly by the Department for Culture Media and Sport (DCMS) until the extension to English Heritage's territorial remit in 2002. There were no sites designated under this Act within the footprint of dredging at the outset of London Gateway, the nearest being the South Edinburgh Channel wreck to the south of Black Deep. Nonetheless, the scope to designate wrecks under the Act – including in an emergency – was acknowledged. Whilst there were wrecks in the wetside area that were likely to be eligible for designation under the Act – notably the *London* (Site 5019/5029)– there had seemed to be no particular merit in doing so because of the PLA's control over activities throughout the Thames. The Act provides for activities on wreck sites to be restricted, and it has been used principally as a means of preventing unauthorised activities by recreational divers or would-be salvors, and to regulate archaeological activities on those sites by providing licences to competent individuals and teams. Of itself, the Act does not denote or confer importance; it is possible for a wreck to be 'important' but not designated.

Equally, archaeological activities connected with development can be regulated through the planning process, either in terms of their adequacy where works are pre-consent, or in terms of conditions on the consent once it has been granted. Although to some extent dependent on voluntary agreement, the investigation of the Gresham Ship in Princes Channel (Auer and Firth 2007) was considered to have shown how a planning-based approach could have a reasonable outcome.

Matters took a different turn, however, when several bronze cannon were salvaged from the *London* and reported to the Receiver of Wreck (Fig. 6). This action was entirely legal; unless a site is designated there is no general prohibition on taking things from it, irrespective of its age. Moreover, the salvage law which applies in such circumstances creates an incentive for such actions to take place, as the law provides that the salvor must receive an award for having carried out salvage, even if the recovered material or the site as a whole deteriorates from having been disturbed. The presence of potentially valuable guns on the *London* was already known (see Part III, below) but the PLA was confident that salvage operations so clearly within its operational area would not be mounted by third parties and the site was not, therefore, at risk. When the recovery of at least two bronze cannon by a private salvage operation showed that this assumption was unfounded, the *London* was designated in October 2008 as a matter of urgency. As the *London* moved into the ambit of site designation, so English Heritage took a more direct role in its management, including carrying out its own investigations of the site both before and after designation. These investigations included diving and desk-based work under the Contract for Archaeological Services in Support of the *Protection of Wrecks Act* 1973 (the PWA Contract), and additional geophysical survey commissioned by English Heritage.

As well as having the potential to be designated, wrecks and their contents continue to be owned despite lying on the seabed for decades or centuries. Whilst the

Figure 6: Cannon salvaged in 2007, at least two confirmed to be from the *London*

individual owners of ships, cargo or personal effects may be lost in time, in many cases ownership is held by organisations that are still current, including the Ministry of Defence and the Department for Transport, which has interests in the remains of merchant ships lost during the two World Wars, for which payment was made under war risks insurance. The interests that such owners continue to have in wreck is one of the reasons underlying the Receiver of Wreck system, as there is a real possibility that recovered wreck will have an owner to which it can be returned. Further, the persistence of ownership in wreck is important for conserving and archiving material of archaeological interest, as ownership of artefacts usually has to be transferred to the receiving museum in order that the artefacts can be properly acquired and accessioned.

The question of original interests in wrecks persisting despite the passage of time is also relevant to a further sensitive issue, which raises important social concerns even if the legal situation is ambiguous. The PMRA 1986, discussed above, was introduced to afford a degree of protection to sites commonly thought of as 'war graves', which it achieves through the designation of selected sites. Whilst the definition of vessels in military service was extended by the courts to encompass some merchant ships, there are very many more vessels lost in

wartime, through military action or otherwise, which are not eligible for designation under the Act. And broader yet than 'war graves' is the question of ships constituting the graves of those who died in the very many collisions, fires, and other casualties that occurred outside of wartime. Many ships have sunk with loss of life and, even if the bodies were washed away or have since decomposed, shipwrecks may be regarded as a last resting place – the only lasting memorial to those who died. As well as being a concern of individuals, especially family members, some organisations place particular emphasis on the need to give due regard to those who died in their service. In the Thames, this is especially true of the importance to Trinity House of the *Argus*, lost to a mine in 1940 with the loss of 34 lives, as discussed below.

Recognising the multiple interests in wrecks likely to be affected by the dredging proposals – particularly ownership and the status of some wrecks as maritime graves – the PLA convened specific meetings in March and December 2006 to exchange information and provide updates. These meetings encompassed the MoD, Department for Transport, Receiver of Wreck, UK Hydrographic Office, Trinity House and English Heritage, as well as the PLA, DP World and Wessex Archaeology.

The wide range of responsibilities and interests in wreck provided the overall context within which the London Gateway investigations developed. However, the immediate prompt – which dominated the earlier phases of investigation – were the processes through which consent for the scheme could be obtained. As a complex and extensive scheme with both dryside and wetside elements, the proposed port required consents under different legal mechanisms. Specifically, consent was sought simultaneously in the forms of an Outline Planning Application (OPA), a Transport and Works Act Order (TWAO) and a Harbour Empowerment Order (HEO), with the marine elements of the scheme largely falling within the scope of the HEO.

Ports are major infrastructure under the terms of the Environmental Assessment Directive; hence the applications had to be accompanied by an EIA. As three applications were being sought, three separate EIAs were developed in parallel, their documentation consistent in format and approach. For the sake of simplicity, and bearing in mind that the investigations discussed here largely fell under the HEO, reference is made in the following paragraphs to a single application/EIA/consent process, which ran up to the Public Inquiry held from February to September 2003.

The Environmental Assessment Directive requires that an EIA addresses archaeological heritage as an aspect of the environment likely to be significantly affected by development. Although transposed into UK law by different regulations, the terminology is consistent so the requirement to address the archaeological heritage is common to the different consent processes. The conduct of EIA including archaeological heritage has been a frequent requirement of major development schemes through the 1990s. On land, EIA was able to build upon the more general approach to archaeology in the planning process that had become established through PPG 16 (Department of the Environment 1990). The approaches taken to archaeology in the course of EIA for the dryside elements of London Gateway were undoubtedly innovative. However, they had the advantage of being able to draw upon increasingly well-established knowledge about the historic environment in the area, an extensive toolbox of existing and developing techniques and practices, a growing body of guidance, and an established curatorial service at both local and national levels.

Marine development schemes had also been subject to the Environmental Assessment Directive, including the requirement to address the archaeological heritage, from exactly the same time as was the case on land. But in 2001 the practical application of EIA to marine archaeology was in a very different state to that on land. As noted above, the planning system did not encompass marine areas, hence the knowledge base, toolbox, guidance and curatorial service had not developed – and were effectively absent at the start. Even with the extension of English Heritage's remit in 2002, specialist input was not available until the consent process was already well developed. As a consequence, the London Gateway development team had to rely largely on its own resources, drawing upon generic principles, some high-level statements, and relatively recent experience from other marine developments. Nonetheless, the extent of London Gateway and the complexity of the Thames' heritage put the scheme in a different league in marine archaeological terms to everything that had gone before.

Environmental impact assessment of the archaeological heritage

The marine archaeological investigations accompanying the consent process spanned the period from April 2001 to the end of the Public Inquiry in September 2003. The key milestones were the submission of applications accompanied by the EIA in July 2002, the submission of additional refinement work in March 2003, and the Public Inquiry which concluded in September 2003.

Wessex Archaeology was first approached in April 2001 to review the results of wetside geotechnical investigations, namely a series of boreholes in the vicinity of the proposed quay and vibrocores along the length of the channel. Geotechnical investigations have the potential to reveal information of archaeological interest about the prehistoric development of the landscape, especially in periods of lower sea level. Such investigations are usually carried out by specialist survey contractors, but it is advantageous for archaeologists to take part so that core material can be observed, recorded and sub-sampled, either when the cores are being recovered from the seabed, or when the samples are being opened or extruded on shore. In the past, the opportunity for direct archaeological observation had often been missed, leaving access just to core logs and disturbed samples, so in this case Royal Haskoning wanted Wessex Archaeology to be involved at an early stage.

Royal Haskoning was prescient in that the geoarchaeological setting of London Gateway Port became a major concern. In due course, Wessex Archaeology was commissioned to review sub-bottom profiler data, to carry out palaeo-geographic mapping of the channel, and to acquire additional sub-bottom survey data. All of this information was drawn upon in developing an integrated deposit model for the new port, focusing in particular on the formerly reclaimed land upon which the majority of the new port was to be sited. Development, evaluation and mitigation based upon the deposit model has formed an important strand of the dryside archaeological investigations, which are published separately (Biddulph *et al.* 2012).

With measures in place to capture the results of on-going geotechnical works, attention switched to Wessex Archaeology's role in the overall development of the EIA for wetside archaeological heritage, working for Royal Haskoning on behalf of P&O, but liaising closely with the dryside archaeology team of Oxford Archaeology working for Oscar Faber, with the Archaeological Liaison Officer providing overall co-ordination.

The need for overall co-ordination was strong, for several reasons. First, as indicated above, the complex scheme cut across different environments and was subject to different consenting paths. Whilst it was sensible to approach wetside and dryside in their own specific terms using appropriate specialists, inconsistency in approach would have made the consent applications vulnerable. Second, there was a desire across the team to achieve an EIA that was archaeologically coherent in research terms. This perspective drew upon experience of another major (though wholly dry) infrastructure scheme – Heathrow Terminal 5 (Framework Archaeology 2010) – which had incorporated an explicit research framework to underpin a selective approach to investigation and mitigation. In the case of a coastal site like London Gateway, it was recognised that the principal classes of archaeological material could only be understood within a framework that accommodated the wetside and the dryside together. Third, notwithstanding the flaws in curatorial infrastructure, the archaeological curators expressed from the outset an expectation that the archaeological approach to London Gateway would be seamless, manifesting a general aspiration arising from initiatives both in the region and elsewhere (Williams and Brown 1999).

A seamless approach to wetside and dryside had a practical expression throughout the EIA process. The section of the Scoping Report in June 2001 on archaeology and cultural heritage combined both wetside and dryside within the same structure. Although more detail was available for the dryside, a preliminary scoping desk study had been carried out for the wetside. It was noted that the potential impact of capital dredging had yet to be established because the location and extent of capital dredging was still being established, but commitments were made to carrying out further work to evaluate the archaeological potential of the wetside and to assess impacts. It was proposed that field evaluation, including diving, would take place following submission of the EIA but in advance of planning consent being granted.

One clear example of the integrated approach to wetside and dryside is that a single database was created to encompass both sets of sites, with a common structure and lexicon. To facilitate day-to-day recording, the number blocks for records on the wetside and dryside were split. Dryside records started at 1000, wetside records at 5000. The unique numbers that began to be allocated to sites at this stage have persisted, which is why many of the wrecks referred to in this volume are coded 5xxx. (Sites first identified on the basis of geophysical data were numbered in a block starting at 7000 hence some of the sites are coded 7xxx).

As indicated above, there was relatively little external guidance from which the method and content of the wetside archaeology EIA could be based. Lack of guidance was a concern because an EIA has, in effect, to meet two tests. The first, more obvious test is that the assessment has to identify significant adverse effects and the measures necessary to mitigate such effects. Of more concern in this case is the second test, which is that the EIA has to be adequate in terms of the methodologies employed in identifying and assessing impacts. That is to say, irrespective of what an assessment concludes about the effects of a scheme, an EIA might fail because the methodologies are considered to have been inadequate.

The notion that an application could be at risk if preparatory investigations are not adequate parallels important policy statements in paragraphs 21 and 22 of PPG 16:

'... it is reasonable for the planning authority to request the prospective developer to arrange for an archaeological field evaluation to be carried out before any decision on the planning application is taken... Local planning authorities can expect developers to provide the results of such assessments and evaluations as part of their application for sites where there is a good reason to believe there are remains of archaeological importance... authorities will need to consider refusing permission for proposals which are inadequately documented.'

The lack of explicit guidance in respect of marine development, exacerbated by limited curatorial expertise at the time, meant that it was up to the development team to posit what would be adequate, at the risk of the EIA (and therefore the application) being undermined if, on submission, a contrary view (from a curator or third party objector) prevailed.

Consequently, the archaeological team was advising P&O both on the likely effects of the scheme, and on the likely adequacy of the EIA methodologies being adopted. As the success of the application – bearing in mind the level of investment involved – turned on this advice, there were risks also to the members of the archaeological team. At the same time, more cautious approaches to assessment were potentially inconsistent with the anticipated timetable for submission, costly, and capable of creating unwelcome precedents for future marine development in the port sector and elsewhere. Moreover, overly cautious methodologies could prove unreasonable and unnecessary if the curators proved to regard them merely as 'desirable' rather than 'essential'.

The existing precedents were limited both in number and in their direct relevance to London Gateway. The overall approach to London Gateway as a major infrastructure project could draw on the experience of schemes such as Heathrow Terminal 5, noted above, but these were overwhelmingly land-based projects. The closest marine parallel in the UK was the EIA for Dibden Terminal, another major port, in Southampton Water. Archaeology at Dibden had been successfully steered through the consent process, such that archaeological concerns had been signed off with the agreement of national and local curators before the Public Inquiry started. Consent was, however, refused on other grounds so the value of the archaeological approach to Dibden Terminal was unproved. Archaeological input to other marine EIAs in the mid–late 1990s was otherwise concerned largely with marine aggregate dredging, far offshore from concentrations of historic shipping such as characterise the Thames, and with much greater scope to avoid impacts by placing exclusion zones around known wrecks.

To the extent that an overall approach to major infrastructure projects had emerged, it placed emphasis on non-intrusive methods for the purposes of the EIA, with any necessary intrusive works to be deferred until consent had been achieved, secured by a condition on the consent. This could be seen as conflicting with the policy set out in PPG 16 quoted above, requiring 'field evaluation to be carried out before any decision'. However, paragraph 21 PPG 16 stated that:

> 'this sort of evaluation is quite distinct from full archaeological excavation. It is normally *a rapid and inexpensive operation*, involving ground survey and small-scale trial trenching' (emphasis added).

In the case of marine works, field evaluation of any sort was unlikely to be inexpensive and the expenditure would be wasted if – as in the case of Dibden Terminal – consent was not granted.

The case could also be made that intrusive evaluation might have the effect of disturbing archaeological sites which, if consent were not granted, would be contrary to the emphasis on avoiding disturbance and preservation *in situ*. On the other hand, curators could maintain that they may not be able to make decisions about ('determine') applications if they had insufficient information available to them, especially if the application area might include a 'showstopper' – nationally important archaeological remains for which there should be a presumption in favour of their physical preservation.

For Dibden Terminal, investigations accompanying the EIA had included desk-based studies, land-based non-intrusive geophysical investigations, walkover surveys in intertidal areas, archaeological interpretation of marine geophysical and geotechnical investigations undertaken for engineering purposes, some limited archaeological diving work, and archaeological evaluation (by trenching) of one wreck discovered in the intertidal area in the course of the other work. Although extensive, it was recognised that all the archaeological concerns at Dibden could not be resolved prior to construction without intrusive work that would be both costly and technically difficult. Equally, the curators were concerned to ensure that if such work were only to take place *after* consent, there would be a mechanism to ensure that the results of intrusive evaluation could inform the development of specific mitigation measures in a way that could be enforced. As a result, the EIA for Dibden Terminal was supported by a Written Scheme of Investigation (WSI) agreed with the curators and

invoked by the consent. The WSI provided both for further evaluation works and for the development of specific mitigation works to be informed by the evaluation. This meant that costly evaluation could be deferred post-consent, whilst ensuring that mitigation would be informed by the results.

Critically, the 'EIA plus WSI' package had the effect that the adequacy of EIA methodologies depended to some degree on the adequacy of the approach to post-consent evaluation and mitigation set out in the WSI. If the WSI was not acceptable then the EIA would not be adequate, as the level of evaluation would be insufficient to allow determination. This added an extra dimension to the EIA process. Conventionally, the EIA seeks to offer mitigation for the significant effects that have already been identified; in the new scenario, the proposed mitigation also played a role in establishing the adequacy of the EIA methodology. In short, concerns about whether the EIA for London Gateway would prove adequate rested not only on the consideration of significant effects, but also to the likely adequacy of evaluation and mitigation.

A further concern – to members of the archaeological team if not more widely – was the commercial risk to the project if a significant archaeological site were to be discovered once dredging had already started. The discovery of such a site would interrupt the dredging programme at the very least, requiring that dredgers be moved whilst the 'obstruction' was addressed. Although some commentators are blithe about the ability of modern dredgers to 'cope with' old wrecks, some such wrecks are surprisingly solid despite their age, and they will resist dredging equipment. In particular, trailer suction dredgers (of the sort likely to be employed on the majority of London Gateway dredging) are generally not capable of removing anything larger than 200–300mm square on account of a mesh across the draghead that prevents debris, including old ordnance, entering the pump. Debris simply gathers on the mesh and obstructs it, requiring the draghead to be cleared. Even more consequentially, discovery of an archaeological site during dredging could require additional works to inspect, evaluate and mitigate the impacts, introducing both delays and extra costs, not only in the dredging programme but also subsequently for recording and analysis (Adams *et al.* 1990). As archaeologists in the EIA team are responsible for advising the developer about the archaeological heritage in the development area, such archaeologists may be vulnerable to redress if they do not advise the developer adequately about what is or may be present, irrespective of the requirements of EIA and consent.

The work carried out in connection with the EIA comprised five main strands, as follows:

- The original EIA, submitted July 2002;
- Refinement of the EIA to reflect changes in the footprint of the channel and additional investigations, submitted March 2003;
- A high-level Port Appraisal;

- Preparation of the Archaeological Mitigation Framework (AMF), which served as the Written Scheme of Investigation to accompany the EIA;
- Negotiation of Statements of Common Ground/Memoranda of Understanding with local and national curators.

These different strands were not prompted primarily by concerns about marine archaeology. They arose from the needs of the EIA and regulatory processes applicable to such a major infrastructure project. The dryside archaeology was also a major and complex concern in its own right, and was a significant driver in the approach that was adopted, drawing – as noted above – from the experience of Heathrow Terminal 5 (Framework Archaeology 2010). For example, the AMF, prepared in parallel with the EIA and serving as the Written Scheme of Investigation, had an explicitly selective approach informed by a research framework, as at Terminal 5, which in the case of London Gateway encompassed both the dryside and the wetside of the project.

Applications for major infrastructure schemes such as London Gateway are often subject to Public Inquiry, in which the developer's plans and EIA are scrutinised in the light of objections raised by government agencies, interest groups and members of the public in front of a Planning Inspector. The Planning Inspector takes all the evidence presented and makes a recommendation to the regulator (Government Minister) who determines the application. Statements of Common Ground (SoCG) and Memoranda of Understanding (MoU) are means of narrowing down – by negotiation and mutual agreement – the scope of the Public Inquiry with respect to a particular topic, setting out the principles and facts that do not need to be examined at Public Inquiry because agreement between the developer and the local and national curators has already been achieved. The AMF provided a focus for the negotiation of the SoCG and MoU and was appended to the final SOCG/MoU. The AMF was submitted as Appendix T of the EIA refinement work.

The July 2002 EIA was predominantly a desk-based exercise, collating information on maritime sites from the National Monuments Record (NMR) and UK Hydrographic Office, and developing an overall narrative of sea-use in the Thames from published and documentary sources. The July 2002 EIA included an extensive gazetteer and GIS-based mapping. A distinction was drawn between actual features on the seabed, and documented losses of ships for which no known remains had been confirmed. As these recorded losses, referred to as 'casualties', have no known remains, they are mapped in the NMR by reference to 'named locations' – predominantly navigational features such as channels and banks – on the basis of the description of the loss in the documentary record. Casualties provide an indication of the potential for as yet unknown wrecks to be discovered, as well as indicating overall patterning of historical sea-use.

The refinement work included a review of sidescan data acquired in 2001, together with a new sidescan and magnetometer survey carried out in 2002. The refinement work also included reworking of the July 2002 EIA to reflect changes in the 'red line' that defined that the maximum footprint of the scheme.

Further work was also carried out in the course of developing the AMF, in the context of negotiating the SoCG/MoU, reflecting on-going discussions about potential impacts and how best they might be evaluated and mitigated. Additional archive research was carried out on the known wrecks, and marine evaluation and mitigation procedures in other countries were reviewed.

Several key points were the subject of considerable debate in the course of the EIA, all set, as indicated previously, against the difficulty and high cost of working in the Thames, and the lack of guidance or curatorial direction about what would constitute a reasonable or adequate EIA. These points were as follows:

- Historical channel dredging and continuing archaeological potential;
- Scope for redesign to avoid impacts to known sites;
- The archaeological character of anomalies;
- The importance of archaeological features.

As outlined above, only limited dredging was required for the navigational channel in its outer reaches, because over large distances the seabed is already deeper than required. Extensive dredging was necessary, however, in the inner reaches of the Thames in an area shown on the charts as the Yantlet Dredged Channel, an area covering approximately 300m wide by 27km long (including 'Sea Reach' extending up to London Gateway Port). The Yantlet is marked on charts as having defined edges and it is known to have been subject to high volumes of dredging in previous decades. Accordingly, it was contended that any archaeological material in the Yantlet must already have been removed and that the scope for impacts from further dredging was very limited. This point of view was important because it had a direct bearing on decisions about how much field investigation was necessary: if previous dredging had removed all the archaeological material, then there was no point in commissioning expensive surveys to see what was (not) there. There are cases where this may be true, where a new channel has been cut deeply into geological strata. However, despite being referred to as a 'dredged channel' the Yantlet is predominantly naturally-formed, and the assumption that previous dredging had removed any archaeological material that might have been present was not sustainable.

The reference to a channel being dredged or maintained need not imply that the whole of the base of the channel has been cleared, merely that high spots have been removed within the maintained area. Even then, areas that have been dredged will only have been cut to the depth required, and any archaeological

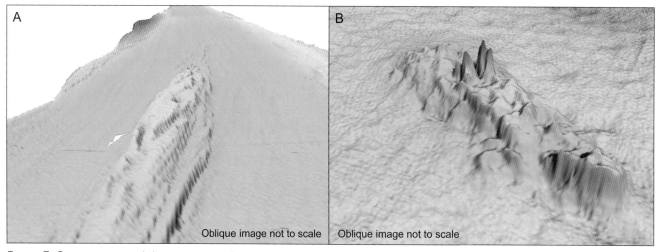

Figure 7: Comparative multibeam images of (A) a natural rock outcrop and (B) a shipwreck

material buried beneath that level could have survived. Often, accounts of historical dredging are quite poorly documented, so that it is difficult to know precisely where dredging took place and what methods were used. Detailed examination of historical and modern charts – comparing depths to a common datum – showed that many metres of material had indeed been removed from the Yantlet but only in a limited area on the edge of the channel. Moreover, the continued presence of many charted wrecks and obstructions strongly suggested that the base of the channel was far from 'clean'. The conclusion of these discussions was that the (lack of) archaeological potential in the Yantlet could not be assumed; it would have to be demonstrated.

Typically, it is preferable to seek to redesign aspects of a marine scheme to avoid impacts to known archaeological sites, because of the general presumption in favour of preservation *in situ* of important sites, and because of the difficulty and cost of investigating such sites and providing mitigation. In the case of London Gateway, there were three known sites at the edge of the proposed channel: the 17th-century warship, *London* (Site 5029); the more extensive remains of a wreck known at the time as the 'King' from which a 17th-century cannon had been recovered (Site 5019); and the 'Iron Bar Wreck' (Site 5020) which, as least superficially, had parallels with the 16th-century Gresham Ship found in the outer Thames (Auer and Firth 2007). As all three sites lay close to the edge of the Yantlet channel there was a strong archaeological case for modifying the line of the proposed dredging to avoid direct impacts, otherwise evaluation and mitigation of each site was likely to prove very costly. Capital dredging schemes are, however, not very flexible in terms of design because of the specifications required in order to achieve safe navigation of very large ships. Even the process of redesigning a section of the channel could be costly and time-consuming, potentially changing the scope of environmental studies already underway and jeopardising the overall timetable of EIA and consent. Consequently, at the EIA stage, the channel was regarded as not capable of alteration to

avoid these specific archaeological impacts. Equally, ballpark figures for proper evaluation and mitigation of the likely effects – encompassing fieldwork, post-fieldwork and material conservation – seriously affected the tone of discussions.

Equally challenging were discussions about the archaeological character of the many indeterminate features on the bed of the channel. The seabed is a messy place, especially in places that have been as heavily used as the Thames. All sorts of debris lost at the surface can accumulate, ranging from whole ships and aircraft to individual items. Once on the seabed such items are affected by a wide range of process that cause them to degrade, collapse, be moved around, mixed up, buried, exposed, and so on. Some of these processes are natural, but others are anthropogenic. In particular, wrecks have been subject to salvage to recover their contents and – more commonly – 'clearance' to reduce the danger that they pose to continuing navigation. Fishing activity can move things around, as well as adding lost gear to the debris. In other cases material has been put into the sea, either to form useful structures or as a means of disposal. In the Thames, this debris has been accumulating and changing over millennia, so a proportion of it is likely to be of archaeological interest and importance, whereas other material is likely to be considered junk (of which more below).

Were this to occur on land, it might be relatively straightforward to carry out a 'walkover' amongst the material and make decisions about what was present and how it should be addressed, aided by historic maps and old air photographs to understand the history of individual features and their context. Under the sea, with negligible visibility, however, such a 'walkover' is unfeasible over such large extents. Previous mapping is relatively coarse and there are no historic photographs of the seabed, whilst background records are essentially anecdotal accounts of chance encounters – where fishermen have snagged their nets or clearance work has been carried out – or are based on hydrographic surveys using the echoes of sound waves to identify possible high spots.

Trying to understand what is on the seabed based on indirect evidence is very difficult. Even where PLA divers had examined features on the seabed, the few lines of recorded observations could be difficult to assess archaeologically. Hence, relative to other stretches of water, the Thames had a good record of the presence of 'things' on the seabed but it was not necessarily clear what they were. Desk-based review showed that there were many known features whose archaeological character was ambiguous: many sites were referred to simply as 'foul', 'obstruction', 'debris', 'feature' or 'unknown'.

The difficulty of distinguishing which features might be of archaeological interest is compounded by the presence of features that cause similar traces but are 'natural' in origin (Fig. 7). For example, outcrops of harder substrate, bedforms and natural changes in sediment can cause fouls, obstructions and anomalies, as can scars caused by fishing gear or anchoring. It has to be borne in mind, however, that 'natural' anomalies may also be caused by the presence of archaeological features at bed level that are, themselves, not visible.

When geophysical data – sidescan and magnetometer – were interpreted, it gave a much clearer and comprehensive view, indicating form, extent, height, character of surrounding seabed, relation to any adjacent features, and magnetic signature. But such geophysical techniques have their own limitations, and are also indirect, requiring interpretation of echoing sound or magnetic fields. As anticipated, geophysical data also showed that there were very many more features on the seabed than evident from previous hydrographic records derived predominantly from single-beam echo-sounders, so whilst it undoubtedly helped in resolving the character of some sites, it also added considerably to the list of features that were ambiguous. The consequence, therefore, of both desk-based and geophysical investigations for the EIA was the recording of very many features on the seabed that might be of archaeological origin, whilst acknowledging that many might turn out to be of no interest at all.

In order to convey the assessment of character in a simple and standardised manner, records were attributed an anthropogenic ('Anthro') rating: 'High', 'Medium', or 'Low'. Items ascribed to the High category were thought very likely to have been created or caused by human activity. Medium and Low denoted increasing uncertainty, for whilst items rated Low appeared more likely to be natural in origin than artificial, the possibility of archaeological interest could not be excluded. By way of example, unprepossessing geophysical returns in the vicinity of a site recorded by the PLA as an 'Ancient Wreck' subject to clearance in the 1960s (Site 5185) were categorised Low in terms of their anthropogenic rating as there was no hint of structure, form or isolated features that might hint at a wreck. This did not mean that there was no wreck present, only that the traces on the seabed did not seem to be artificial. In contrast, some of the features rated High were quite obviously artificial but – in the case of moorings for

navigational buoys, for example – it was equally obvious that they were of little archaeological interest. The 'Anthro' rating was not, therefore, a measure of *importance*, and although it offered a simple grading that was attractive in preparing the EIA, the caveat that High could be unimportant whilst Low could be important caused confusion.

The question of archaeological importance is central to the EIA process because the significance of effects attributable to a proposed scheme is usually gauged by considering the magnitude of impacts against the importance of the feature ('receptor') subject to those impacts. However, ascribing archaeological importance has a subjective element, so the boundary between archaeologically-important material and junk is not based only on physical facts. Not everything that is old is important, whilst some things that are relatively young can be highly important.

Where the archaeological character of a feature is itself uncertain, it is difficult to be anything but vague about its possible importance on the basis of indirect evidence alone. A foul, obstruction or anomaly of uncertain origin could prove to be very important; but it could also prove to be just rubbish. However, even where the character was more certain, assigning importance could be equally problematic. Whilst there were some known sites that were clearly important, their overall number was quite small. There was a much larger number of known sites whose importance, being subjective, was open to debate – especially smaller wooden vessels likely to be of late 19th- or 20th-century date, and ships (eg merchant ships and small warships) lost in the 20th century. At the time of the EIA there was no formal guidance about importance that could be readily applied. Traditionally, such wrecks have been regarded as unimportant, subject to clearance and disposal with negligible archaeological input. However, broadly equivalent industrial and military monuments on land were subject to much higher levels of investigation and protection, and comparable vessels that have been preserved afloat could be found on lists such as the National Register of Historic Vessels. In some cases there was clear social interest in some of the wreck sites, especially where there had been loss of life, but such interest did not necessarily fall within the ambit of assessing the archaeological heritage.

Archaeological importance was rated – as 'Low', 'Medium', 'High', 'Very High' or 'Uncertain', and sometimes as a range (eg 'Uncertain, possibly High or Very High'; 'Uncertain possibly Low'). As noted above, there could be apparent clashes with the High-Medium-Low 'Anthro' rating. The overall theme was of considerable uncertainty!

The only means of distinguishing which items were of archaeological origin, and then which of these was of archaeological importance, would be to send divers – preferably archaeologists – down to the features to enable their evaluation. Given the scale of the scheme and the timescale for the EIA, the prospect of costly diving operations was not especially welcome. Two

Stage I Mitigation	A	Documentary investigation to establish relative importance.
	B	Archaeological inspection by diver and/or remote operated vehicle (ROV) to prove/disprove their character by direct observation.
	C	Site-specific multibeam bathymetric survey to quantify site topography.
	D	Site-specific geophysical survey comprising sub-bottom and magnetometer survey to establish extents of buried/ferrous material.
	E	Intrusive investigation to gauge the complexity of stratigraphy, survival of artefacts, conservation needs and coherence of structural remains.
Stage II Mitigation	F	Avoidance, to include monitoring.
	G	Dispersal/clearance without further archaeological recording.
	H	Controlled dispersal/clearance, ie with limited archaeological observation and recording in the course of dispersal/recovery operations.
	I	Archaeological recording (to include limited excavation) prior to controlled dispersal/clearance, recovery being limited to finds rather than structure.
	J	Archaeological recovery, ie recording (to include excavation) and recovery of all or part of the wreck structure and its contents.
Stage III Mitigation	K	Mechanisms for reporting, assessing/evaluating and managing sites uncovered by construction.
	L	Periodic inspection of the base and sections of dredged areas, to include assessing/evaluating and managing sites that are uncovered.
	M	Periodic survey of areas (eg channel sides) where sediment movement occurs following dredging or following increases in size and volume of traffic, to include assessing/evaluating and managing sites that are uncovered.

Table 1: Stages of post-consent investigation

avenues were pursued: the first was to categorise the anomalies into types of which a sample could be evaluated by diving, in order to provide feedback to assessment of the whole; the second was to develop a staged approach to further investigation that would be deferred post-consent, allowing the uncertainties to be resolved and appropriate mitigation provided once it was known that the scheme could go ahead. Although the typology of anomalies was developed, diving to sample the anomaly types did not take place. However, the staged approach proposed for post-consent investigations (Table 1) provided a framework for all subsequent work in the pre-clearance, clearance and dredging stages of the scheme.

The EIA made best use of the extensive investigations that had been undertaken up to that point, but without all of the issues being fully resolved. No objection was raised by local or national curators in respect of the wetside, and the subject was not examined at the Public Inquiry which finished in September 2003. The Inspector's Report was submitted to the Secretary

of State for Transport in February 2004. In July 2005 the Secretary of State formally stated that he was 'minded to grant' consent, subject to resolution of some remaining issues. Hence the EIA, uncontested on marine archaeology, appeared to achieve a reasonable and adequate balance, but some of the points of contention that had not been resolved were to resurface again.

Development of mitigation proposals

With receipt of a 'minded to grant' letter from the Secretary of State in July 2005, attention switched to some of the practical implications of the scheme going ahead, although negotiations over road links meant that consent was only granted formally in May 2007. In the meantime, it had been decided that the PLA would undertake some works necessary to improve navigation under its own statutory powers, in preparation for London Gateway dredging that would be carried out once consent was received (Fig. 8).

The main preparatory work was to be clearance of a list of known obstructions – including a number of large wrecks – that coincided with some of the sites addressed in the wetside archaeological assessment. It was recognised by the PLA that this clearance would have to take account of the archaeological considerations set out in respect of the dredging scheme, and that a range of archaeological actions would need to be carried out prior to clearance taking place (ie pre-clearance). Accordingly, Wessex Archaeology was approached by the PLA in August 2005 to prepare mitigation assessments for wrecks in the channel, building on experience from the Gresham Ship, and on work by Wessex Archaeology for the PLA on its overall strategy towards the potential archaeological importance of wrecks within the PLA's jurisdiction.

By this stage, part of the channel had been redesigned so that the three sites of great concern during the EIA would not be impacted directly by dredging. The changes to the proposed dredging work to secure preservation *in situ* of three sites thought to be of considerable archaeological significance was a major success arising out of the earlier work. As a further sign of the profile that archaeology had gained, the PLA had also started to carry out its own programme of survey and dive inspection on known seabed features in the Yantlet. This work included archaeological inspections by Nigel Nayling of University of Wales Trinity Saint David, Lampeter (Nayling 2005a–b).

The initial work by Wessex Archaeology for the PLA comprised correlation of all the available datasets relative to the proposed extent and depth of dredging, using GIS and an accompanying database. As well as work carried out in the EIA, the current version of the PLA's own wreck database was incorporated, together with multibeam surveys and dive reports undertaken by the PLA. All of the available information was reviewed – including sidescan data from 2001 and 2003 – and each site was ascribed to a 'mitigation group'.

Figure 8: Dredging in progress

Aside from removing some duplicate records arising from the use of multiple sources, the features were split into three main groups:

- Non-relevant sites;
- Sites of Certain, Probable or Possible Archaeological Interest;
- Uncertains.

The sites classified as 'Non-relevant' included features that were clearly of no archaeological interest – predominantly moorings for navigational buoys, sites that had already been cleared, sites that fell outside the footprint of the channel and side slopes, and sites that were within the footprint but the seabed depth was already below the proposed dredging depth.

The sites of 'Certain, Probable or Possible Archaeological Interest' were categorised as in Table 2. These categories – Certain, Probable and Possible – still grappled with the uncertainty about the character of material on the seabed, and about its importance. The 'Probable' category accommodated sites where remains were certain, but their importance less clear – such as the *Dovenby* (Sites 5010/5012) and the Brick Barge (Site 5230); and sites whose importance would be clear if material proved to be present – such as the elusive 'Ancient Wreck' (Sites 5185/7609) recorded in the PLA database but not yet re-located. The categorisation acknowledged that uncertainty about the degree of importance was attributable in part to the point-of-view of the person making the evaluation, in the continuing absence of curatorial guidance.

Certain	Used for the small number of sites that are clearly of archaeological interest, with remains present on the seabed that are likely to be considered of high importance.
Probable	Used for sites where there are certainly remains present which are likely to be considered at least moderately important, plus sites where the presence of remains is less certain, but if present the remains will be considered of moderate to high importance.
Possible	Generally used for sites where there are certainly remains present, where those remains may be of low to moderate importance, or important to a specific sector. This category largely comprises known wrecks lost in WWI and WWII ... As above, the level of importance will depend on the details of the site, and may be debated.

Table 2: Categorisation of Sites of Certain, Probable or Possible Archaeological Interest

The 'Uncertains' were also split into sub-categories, as shown in Table 3. The attribution of the 'Uncertains' to these sub-categories was based on professional judgement, acknowledging that any of the 'Uncertains' could prove to be archaeological in origin.

The dredge as a whole was split into two regions: one corresponding roughly to the Yantlet above (upstream of) the navigational buoy Sea Reach 1 to London Gateway port; the other region being below Sea Reach 1, down the Estuary and out into the North Sea. The results of the attribution of sites to mitigation groups are shown in Table 4.

Uncertain – ?bed feature	On the basis of the sidescan images, these sites seem likely to be bed features (sand banks, sand waves, disturbance to bed caused by trawling, anchoring etc.). This interpretation draws on the form of the anomaly and the character of the surrounding seabed.
Uncertain – ?debris	These can be reasonably interpreted as artificial, ie of human origin, but are more likely to be 'modern' than of archaeological origin or interest. This group includes linears (?lost chains and cables) and generally isolated single items. It should be noted that some of these isolated items may prove to be quite old and of some archaeological interest, but as they seem to be isolated depositions they will not have much in the way of context. It should also be noted that the features identified as debris may need to be cleared to facilitate dredging.
Uncertain – ambiguous	These are features that cannot be ascribed to another group. They may prove to be of archaeological importance, but they may prove to be modern, or even natural in origin.
Uncertain – ?archaeological feature	These seem reasonably likely – on the basis of currently available data – to have an archaeological origin, or at least to be a class of anomalies that includes features of archaeological origin and importance. They can be reasonably interpreted as being artificial, and are either more extensive than 'debris' or are made up of several elements. This classification does not consider the level of importance that might apply – ie some of these features may prove to be of archaeological origin, but of low importance. However, some of them may prove to be of high importance. These attributions have been made while bearing in mind that some of the most important sites (prehistoric, Roman, medieval) may be very ephemeral.

Table 3: Categories of Uncertains

It is worth noting that the significant difference in numbers, especially for 'Uncertains', between Above SR1 and Below SR1 is likely to be a consequence of the higher resolution sidescan survey in 2002 only being carried out in the Yantlet. The data available below Sea Reach 1 – obtained in 2001 – were of much lower resolution, so it is likely that the small features that make up many of the 'Uncertains' would not have been visible in the sidescan data.

This process drew attention to the relatively small number of 'Certain, Probable and Possible' sites. This number was further reduced in that some individual sites were clearly associated with others and could be grouped. For example, the *Dovenby* (Site 5010/5012) had a number of outlying anomalies that were likely to be debris from its original wrecking or subsequent clearance, and the Anti-submarine Boom (Site 5195) was made up of numerous individually identifiable elements.

The sites identified as 'Certain, Probable and Possible' were allocated to the staged approach to post-consent investigations developed during the EIA, highlighting the forms of investigation necessary in order to inform decisions about mitigation, and the likely mitigation process. As noted, some sites were to be avoided, whereas others required further survey or inspection.

In order to provide a focus for further investigation and mitigation, a new form of document was developed known as a Clearance Mitigation Statement (CMS). Up to this point, sites had been dealt with collectively, as an aspect of the London Gateway scheme as a whole. The CMSs were site-specific, concentrating narrowly on the characteristics and requirements of the individual site in its own terms, though still drawing upon the overall categorisations of mitigation group and mitigation stages to maintain consistency of approach. The original list of CMSs, corresponding to 47 'Certain, Probable and Possible' sites, is shown in Table 5.

The CMSs were also expected to be 'living' documents in the sense that they would be updated with the results of further investigations and decision-making as the scheme progressed. They would be prepared in the pre-clearance phase with the intention of having a complete document to inform the clearance phase itself, to sign-off the site for clearance with all archaeological work already completed pre-clearance, or setting out the details of any remaining mitigation that would take place during clearance.

Each CMS included the following:

- A summary of the survey history of the site;
- A description of the site based on survey data;
- An account of the history of the vessel or structure based on Wessex Archaeology's build-use-loss model Reference – *On the Importance of Shipwrecks* project for ship narratives (Wessex Archaeology 2006a);
- Its perceived importance;
- Details of any known constraints such as the possible presence of ordnance or human remains;
- And an outline of the further investigations and anticipated mitigation process that would apply.

Mitigation proposals were framed as a series of options (see Table A1) that were incorporated into the AMF, and related to Wessex Archaeology's system of recording levels (see Table 6) to ensure that recording objectives for the sites remained transparent. Where previous PLA diving had included an archaeological element, the report from Nigel Nayling (2005a–b) was appended. Each CMS was illustrated with the results of survey data and photographs, where available.

Sites were added and removed, and names changed, in the light of new evidence or changes to proposals, but altogether CMSs were prepared for each of the 29 entries in Table 7.

The CMSs were prepared between January 2006 and August 2008. Based initially on desk-based sources (including the results of PLA survey and diving, as well as Wessex Archaeology's EIA work), they were

	Above SR1	Below SR1	Total
Duplicates total	-	-	**19**
Non-relevant total	-	-	**202**
Features of no archaeological interest	-	-	28
Site clear	-	-	22
Beyond channel	-	-	128
Below dredge depth	-	-	24
Certains, Probables and Possibles total	**34**	**13**	**47**
Sites of certain archaeological interest	3	0	3
Sites of Probable archaeological interest	23	5	28
Sites of Possible archaeological interest	8	8	16
Uncertains total	**267**	**58**	**325**
Uncertain – bed feature	21	3	24
Uncertain – debris	106	11	117
Uncertain – ambiguous	69	2	71
Uncertain – ?archaeological feature	71	42	113
Total			**593**

Table 4: Attribution of sites to mitigation groups
(SR= sea reach)

augmented over the period with additional geophysical data, documentary research, and the results of archaeological diving investigations.

The key geophysical data adding to the CMSs were high resolution multibeam acquired by the PLA, using an 8125 Reson SeaBat installed permanently in the PLA survey vessel *Yantlet*. The data were acquired by the PLA in the course of their overall survey programmes, and the data were passed to Wessex Archaeology for processing and interpretation. As well as providing very useful quantitative information in their own right, the multibeam data were interpreted in conjunction with previously obtained sidescan data, and formed a GIS layer for subsequent diving investigations.

Additional documentary research focused on the named wrecks, to better understand their history and potential importance. Research was carried out at the National Archives and National Maritime Museum, and included obtaining ship plans, photographs and first-hand accounts of wrecking incidents. The documentary research added considerably to understanding the social history associated with the wartime wrecks in particular, and helped clarify questions about the potential for human remains and ordnance which were also of wider concern.

In operational terms, archaeological diving investigations took two main forms: first, operations conducted by a team made up wholly of Wessex Archaeology diving archaeologists; second, operations conducted principally by PLA divers with Wessex Archaeology diving archaeologists embedded within the PLA team. Additionally, the PLA conducted its own diving operations, as a result of which information was passed to Wessex Archaeology (Table 8).

Diving operations were linked directly to the CMSs, specifically in the need for further information to inform mitigation options in the CMSs. Diving was to take place in two stages (I and II).

CMS	Mitigation group	WA_ID	Site name
Above Sea Reach 1			
'King'	Certain	5019	*'King'*
London	Certain	5029	*London* (possibly)
'Pottery Wreck'	Certain	5204	Unknown ('Pottery Wreck')
Dovenby	Probable	5010	*Dovenby* (S Part)
		5012	*Dovenby* (N Part)
		7368	Unknown (?*Dovenby*)
		7369	Unknown (?*Dovenby*)
		7370	Unknown (?*Dovenby*)
		7371	Unknown (?*Dovenby*)
		7139	Unknown (?*Dovenby*)
		7140	Unknown (?*Dovenby*)
		7708	Unknown (?*Dovenby*)
		7709	Unknown (?*Dovenby*)
'Iron Bar Wreck'	Probable	5020	Unknown ('Iron Bar Wreck')
Wreck NW of SR 1	Probable	5046	Unknown (Wreck NW of Sea Reach 1)
		5050	N/A (Aircraft under mound)
		5051	Unknown ('Old Timbers and Concrete')
'Ancient Wreck'	Probable	5185	Unknown ('Ancient Wreck')
		7609	?'Ancient Wreck'
Brick Barge	Probable	5230	Unknown (1019) (Brick Barge)
		7128	Unknown (?Brick Barge)
		7224	Unknown (?Brick Wreck)
		7540	Unknown (?Brick Barge)
		7345	Unknown (disturbed area)
		7404	60m Feature
		7543	Anomaly Cluster
		7563	Complex Anomaly
Anti-submarine Boom	Possible	5195	Unknown (?Anti-submarine boom)
		7476	?Anti-submarine Boom
		7477	?Anti-submarine Boom
		7478	?Anti-submarine Boom
		7544	?Anti-submarine Boom
		7546	?Anti-submarine Boom
		7547	?Anti-submarine Boom
		7586	?Anti-submarine Boom
Below Sea Reach 1			
East Oaze	Probable	5056	East Oaze Light Vessel
		5124	Unknown
		6595	Halcrow A5
Letchworth	Possible	5005	*Letchworth*
Argus	Possible	5008	*Argus*
Atherton	Possible	5011	*Atherton*
Ash	Possible	5013	*Ash*
Unknown Aircraft	Possible	5041	Unknown Aircraft
Amethyst	Possible	5063	HMS *Amethyst*
Ryal	Possible	5070	*Ryal*
		7209	?Debris from *Ryal*
Dynamo	Possible	5100	*Dynamo*

Table 5: Original list of CMSs (ordered by mitigation group)

Level	Type	Objective	Sub-level	Character	Scope	Description
1	Assessment	A record sufficient to establish the presence, position and type of site	1a	Indirect (desk-based)	A basic record based on documentary, cartographic or graphic sources, including photographic (incl. AP), geotechnical and geophysical surveys commissioned for purposes other than archaeology	Documentary assessment/inventory of a site, compiled at the start of work on a site, and updated as work progresses
			1b	Direct (field)	A basic record based on field observation, walkover survey, diving inspection etc., including surveys commissioned specifically for archaeological purposes	Typically a 1–2 dive visit to the site (to assess a geophysical anomaly, etc.)
2	Evaluation	A record that provides sufficient data to establish the extent, character, date and importance of the site	2a	Non-intrusive	A limited record based on investigations that might include light cleaning, probing and spot sampling, but without bulk removal of plant growth, soil, debris etc.	Typically a 2–4 dive visit to assess the site's archaeological potential, backed up by a sketch plan of the site with some key measurements included.
			2b	Intrusive	A limited record based on investigations including vigorous cleaning, test pits and/or trenches. May also include recovery (following recording) of elements at immediate risk, or disturbed by investigation	Either an assessment of the buried remains present on a site; the recovery of surface artefacts; or cleaning to inform, for example, a 2a investigation
3	*In situ*	A record that enables an archaeologist who has not seen the site to comprehend its components, layout and sequences	3a	Diagnostic	A detailed record of selected elements of the site	The first stage of a full record of the site. This would include a full measured sketch of the site and a database (or equivalent) entry for all surface artefacts
			3b	Unexcavated	A detailed record of all elements of the site visible without excavation	Full site plan (ie planning frame or equivalent accuracy) with individual object drawings, and full photo record (possibly including a mosaic)
			3c	Excavated	A detailed record of all elements of the site exposed by open excavation of part or whole of the site	This may take the form of full or partial excavation of a site
4	Removal	A record sufficient to enable analytical reconstruction and/or reinterpretation of the site, its components and its matrix			A complete record of all elements of the site in the course of dismantling and/or excavation	
5	Intra-site	A record that places the site in the context of its landscape and other comparable sites			A complete record of all elements of the site, combined with selective recording of comparable sites and investigation of the surrounding area	

Table 6: Archaeological wreck recording levels

Stage I diving was intended to achieve Level 1b (field assessment – see Table 6) and some aspects of Level 2a (non-intrusive evaluation – see Table 6), and to be brief – 1.5–2 hours of bottom time in each case – bearing in mind the operational difficulties and cost of diving operations in the Thames. Stage I was intended to clarify the characteristics of the site especially where this character – based on geophysical or other indirect information – was ambiguous. Stage I diving would also occur where the character was known but further information was required, notably on some of the identified wrecks lost in wartime with known or suspected loss of life where diving was necessary to indicate the presence of human remains, personal effects, or munitions, all of which could have a bearing on clearance.

Stage II diving was intended to achieve Level 3 (*in situ* recording – see Table 6), and was expected to take significantly more time. However, no diving was planned for sites that were to be avoided by dredging – namely the 'King', 'Iron Bar Wreck' and *London* – and on 20th-century wrecks on which there had been no apparent loss of life.

WA _ID	Site name
5005	*Letchworth*
5008	*Argus*
5010/5012	*Dovenby*
5011	*Atherton*
5013	*Ash*
5019	'King'
5020	'Iron Bar Wreck'
5029	*London*
5041	Unknown Aircraft
5046	Wreck NW of Sea Reach 1
5050	Aircraft/Coal dump
5051	Wreck – Mid-Blyth ('Old Timbers and Concrete')
5056	East Oaze Light Vessel
5057	*Aisha*
5063	*Amethyst*
5070/7209	*Ryal*
5100	*Dynamo*
5124	Possible Wreck
5185/7609	'Ancient Wreck'
5195 etc.	Anti-submarine Boom
5204	'Pottery Wreck'
5230	Brick Barge
5960	*Storm*
5961	*Erna Boldt*
6595	Halcrow A5
7345	Disturbed Area (planking)
7404	60m Feature
7543	Anomaly Cluster (German aircraft)
7563	Complex Anomaly

Table 7: Sites for which CMSs were prepared (ordered numerically)

PLA Diving operations	Spring 2006 onwards
WA Diving operations	Initially planned for May–June 2006; carried out Nov 2007
PLA with WA embedded	18 August 2006 – German Aircraft 7543
	30 October 2007 – *London*, following reports of salvage
	April 2008 – continuation of Nov 2007 assessments (Sites 5029; 5046; 5051; 5124)
	June 2008 – in-water observation and recording on Sites 5051 and 5204

Table 8: Diving investigations

The main phase of Wessex Archaeology diving operations was initially planned for May–June 2006 but eventually took place in November 2007. Operations were planned to take place using a substantial 'live aboard' vessel as a dive platform, partly because of the large amount of transit time that would otherwise be needed if travelling to and from shore each day, given the limited distribution of suitable harbours in the Thames, and partly because of the need to have a substantial vessel when diving in the busy navigational channel. In order to avoid the cost of demobilising and then remobilising a large vessel, Stage II diving was to run directly on from Stage I, with the results of Stage I directly informing the selection of sites for Stage II. As the selection of sites for Stage II would require the agreement of English Heritage in the course of diving operations, a decision tree was prepared in advance that

set thresholds and anticipated outcomes. In the event, diving in November 2007 was severely hampered by poor weather, high tidal ranges (including a record storm surge) and difficulties anchoring in the channel. Of 14 sites planned for diving operations, diving took place on ten. On seven of these, diving was sufficiently conclusive to inform mitigation; in three, diving had been curtailed and there continued to be ambiguity. Four sites were not subject to diving in November 2007, all in the outer Estuary where weather conditions were such that operations were postponed.

The outcome of the main phase of November 2007 diving was that English Heritage agreed that watching briefs would take place during clearance of the Brick Barge (Site 5230) and the site where carvel planking had been recovered (Site 7345). English Heritage agreed that no further archaeological work was necessary on five sites:

- Further diving was required on three sites (Wreck NW of Sea Reach 1 (Site 5046);
- Wreck – Mid-Blyth ('Old Timbers and Concrete') (Site 5051);
- and 'Possible Wreck' (Site 5124), plus the sites in the outer Estuary.

A short time before the November 2007 fieldwork, an unanticipated event took place on the 'King'/*London* sites (Site 5019/5029). A private salvage operation had recovered at least two bronze cannon, and in order to gauge the damage done to the sites by the salvage operation, the PLA carried out its own diving operation with an embedded Wessex Archaeology diver on 30 October 2007. Several artefacts were recovered. The 'King'/*London* sites were subsequently designated under the *Protection of Wrecks Act* 1973.

Wessex Archaeology divers embedded within the PLA diving team became the main mode of diving to complete Stage I, principally in April 2008. Diving was carried out on Sites 5029, 5046, 5051 and 5124. In advance of clearance, in-water observation and recording took place on Sites 5051 and 5024. Finally, Wessex Archaeology attended PLA clearance operations on the *Dovenby* (Sites 5010/5012) and *Aisha* (Site 5057) in connection with filming by Touch Productions on the two-part series *Thames Shipwrecks: a race against time*, which was aired on BBC2 (26 August/2 September 2008) (Fig. 9).

At the same time that fieldwork to support the CMSs was being planned and carried out, attention was also being paid to the documentation that would accompany clearance and, in due course, dredging. Three sets of documentation were prepared:

- *A Protocol for Discoveries during Dredging* was developed by the PLA and agreed with English Heritage. The Protocol provided that known anomalies would be indicated to the dredging contractor, and required that 'strikes' on hitherto unknown archaeological material had to be

Figure 9: Filming in progress for BBC 2's *Thames Shipwrecks: a race against time*

reported to London Gateway, and thence to English Heritage. Recognising that there was still a large number of Uncertains in the vicinity of Sea Reach 1 in particular, the Protocol also provided that a watching brief would be carried out during dredging in that area;

- A document on *Exclusion Zones* and monitoring was prepared by Wessex Archaeology on behalf of the PLA and agreed with English Heritage. Preparation of the document included designing three Exclusion Zones around the sites of the 'Iron Bar Wreck' (Site 5020), 'King'/*London* (Sites 5019/5029), underpinning the mitigation strategy of avoiding these sites by moving the proposed channel. As well as clearly defining areas in which no dredging or ancillary works were to take place, provision was made for periodic monitoring by multibeam survey during and after dredging to indicate any changes to these sites and enable a response;

- A document on *Methods and Procedures* was prepared by Wessex Archaeology on behalf of PLA and agreed with English Heritage, summarising the approach to data and outlining the mitigation strategy to be adopted with respect to each site. The document also included details of the procedures that were to apply in respect of the handling of archaeological material, including ordnance, human remains and 'wreck'.

All three documents were appended to the Dredge Plan, which was attached both to the contract between London Gateway and the dredging company, and to the Tidal Works Agreement between London Gateway and the PLA (as regulator). This meant that the archaeological documentation was enforceable both as part of the dredging contract and as part of the dredging consent.

Dredging started in March 2010 and was still on-going when this volume was being prepared. The results of archaeological investigations associated with dredging, based on the documents listed above, will be published in due course.

Part II
Investigative Methodologies

INTRODUCTION

This section discusses the principal methods of investigation employed by Wessex Archaeology during the London Gateway scheme. This included desk-based methods that examined records of wrecks and obstructions, and casualty data. The whole process involved the generation of digital datasets with a GIS component.

Marine geophysics provides a method to rapidly survey large areas of seabed and complements the traditional diver-based methods that tend to focus on smaller areas and sites. One of the issues of diving in the Thames Estuary is low visibility which presents difficulties when surveying. Geophysics provides many advantages not least a more comprehensive coverage, three-dimensional modelling and intra-site coverage of the position and physical extent of wrecks. These aspects along with the four different types of equipment deployed during the London Gateway project are discussed below. Within the London Gateway project diver-based methods were used to characterise sites and wrecks. A discussion of the methods and issues is presented below.

Desk-based methods

The 'wetside' component of the EIA included a desk-based assessment of sources relevant to the maritime archaeology likely to be encountered within the area affected by the proposed channel dredge (see Part I, above).

The principal sources that were collated, examined and interpreted were the wreck and obstruction records held by the UK Hydrographic Office (UKHO) and the maritime records held by the National Record of the Historic Environment (NRHE). Searches of UKHO wreck and obstruction records for the study area led to the identification of over 200 known wrecks and obstructions. An additional 14 known sites were identified from NRHE records. Taking duplicate records between the two sources into account, a total of 254 wrecks was identified.

Data for each site were obtained directly from the UKHO in the form of full ('long') text-based wreck reports, and from the NRHE in the form of shapefiles and full text reports of each monument record. Both sets of records were transcribed into Excel spreadsheets and thence into shapefiles for GIS analysis. The use of GIS in this respect was a critical aspect of the methodology as it enabled sites within areas likely to be impacted by the dredge to be identified and sorted, and for the changes in the extent of the proposed scheme to be rapidly accounted for, as well as defining the initial data search areas.

The UKHO records are prepared in order to comply with the UKHO's responsibilities towards safety of navigation. They therefore reflect a concern with wrecks as potential navigational hazards rather than as archaeological sites. However, much of the information is directly relevant to archaeological assessment and it is compiled in a way that is largely objective and comparable. For example, UKHO records provide what is usually (but not always) an accurate position, together with maximum and minimum depths that give an indication as to the height of any upstanding wreckage. They give an indication as to the size of the wreck, usually from geophysical survey data, and often categorise condition based on the available evidence, for example 'intact' or 'dispersed'. In addition, they give available information as to the identity of the vessel and its history, including the date and circumstances of loss, as well as information concerning the history of the wreck since the loss occurred, including any recent salvage, clearance and survey that is known to have occurred. This historical information is rarely complete but provides a useful starting point if further research is warranted.

NRHE maritime records of wrecks include both located wreck sites and features regarded as potential wreck sites. Due to the form of its searches, NRHE data were sourced for a far wider area than the wetside study area. To some extent NRHE records incorporate and, therefore, duplicate UKHO records, although they also include available primary and secondary documentary evidence. However, it was notable that 14 wrecks and obstructions that were recorded by the NRHE did not appear in the UKHO searches.

Casualty data are also recorded by the NRHE and were included in the EIA, with a total of 519 relevant casualties identified. Casualties are documented vessel losses for which no wreck site has yet been located. They are typically recorded as having occurred at named locations which are assigned positions by the NRHE on the basis of the location described by the source. Examples of poorly defined locations range from the very vague 'Entrance to the Thames Estuary' to relatively well defined, but extensive and historically shifting locations such as 'Sunk Sand' or 'Long Sand'. As only a single position is assigned to a named location that may cover a large area, casualties that were lost well away from the study area may appear in search results. Equally, casualties may not appear because the assigned position for the location happens to be outside the study area.

Casualty data are relevant to EIA assessments because unidentified wrecks in a study area may be among the recorded casualties and because there may be clues as to the potential for further discoveries of wrecks within the study area, in this case during the subsequent geophysical survey, interpretation of this data, or clearance and dredging. In addition, casualty data play a role in providing a maritime historical context for the known wrecks.

The value of casualty data varies according to the source and date. Documentary data concerning shipping loss prior to the medieval period are almost entirely absent. Records kept of shipping losses prior to the 18th century and, in particular, prior to the introduction of insurance-related records in the mid-18th century are primarily concerned with salvage, and often provide very little useful information, particularly as to the location of the loss. In addition, they are fragmentary and extremely scarce. It is therefore hard to know how representative they are of the scale of losses that occurred. We know from various strands of evidence that the volume of vessel traffic was probably significantly less than it was to become in the 18th and 19th centuries, for example the number of London-owned trading ships increased from about 12,300 tons to about 140,000 tons in the period between 1582 and 1702 (Davis 1962, 35), and it might be concluded that fewer losses might be expected in any event. Nevertheless, common sense suggests that the pre-18th-century records traced for the Thames Estuary are unlikely to provide a reliable guide to the scale of the casualties that actually occurred there.

During the 18th and 19th centuries records gradually improved with respect to larger commercial and military vessels. Centralised casualty records were kept, first by insurers (principally Lloyds of London) and then by government. Nevertheless, wreck reporting remained imperfect until the late 19th century, with a Select Committee appointed to inquire into the causes of shipwreck in 1836 admitting that the data upon which they were forced to deliberate did not 'embrace the whole extent of the loss' (Larn and Larn 1996). By the 20th century casualty reporting of larger vessel losses had become reliable. Nevertheless, the loss of smaller vessels continued to go unrecorded and the crucial location information could still remain somewhat vague.

Data directly from the PLA wreck index was not made available for the EIA, although it was included once work started for the PLA on mitigation and clearance. However, PLA-derived data were present within the UKHO data. Local authority data were not used on the wetside because at the time their marine records drew heavily on national records, exacerbating problems of duplication that would arise with other data sources.

In addition, a variety of other sources were consulted during the EIA, including:

- Records of wreck material salvaged and found held by HM Receiver of Wreck;
- Information received from the Naval Staff Directorate of the Ministry of Defence; and
- Secondary published sources held by local record offices and local museums.

Historical charts, sailing directions and other navigational records held by a variety of organisations were integrated into the initial discussion of archaeological context. Further, more detailed examination illuminated the dredging history of the study area (as has been described elsewhere in this volume), although the extent to which documented historical changes in the position of navigational hazards and shipping routes in the estuary affect the archaeological potential of the study area is a more difficult question to answer, and remains uncertain.

It is important that all of this should be understood in the context of a dynamic process of development in archaeological methodology. The London Gateway EIA was compiled in 2002–3. Although many aspects of the wetside component and of subsequent desk-based work were ground-breaking, practice and guidance in respect of some elements of the EIA have since moved on, partly as a result of the experience generated by this project.

For example, considerable attention was paid in the wetside baseline to a lengthy discussion of the general maritime archaeological context. The increasing numbers of regional environmental assessments and research frameworks available, including the Outer Thames Estuary Regional Environmental Characterisation (REC) (Sturt and Dix 2009), would render some of this discussion unnecessary today. National studies of the impact of navigational hazards on archaeological potential were not available at the time that it was written (Merritt et al. 2007). Far greater emphasis would now be given in the discussion to the post-medieval and modern periods, as it is very clear that vessels from these periods dominate both the archaeological and documentary record of the Thames, and are of increasing concern from a curatorial perspective. Furthermore, it is likely that the casualty data from the NRHE would be far more closely integrated in the discussion of context.

One very notable absence from the discussion of archaeological resources within the initial EIA was aviation. Records of aircraft wreck sites and casualties were included in the GIS and gazetteers, and were assessed and subsequently considered in terms of mitigation, but no account was provided of the general history of aviation activity or potential for other sites to be present. Awareness, or at least acknowledgement, of the potential for aviation archaeology at sea among archaeologists and curators is a relatively new and growing phenomenon. EIAs that paid any or sufficient attention to this issue prior to the publication of English

Heritage's national scoping study on aircraft crash sites at sea in 2008 were relatively few (Wessex Archaeology 2008a). Fortunately this lack of attention does not seem to have impacted upon aviation archaeology within the dredged channel. The single aircraft crash site subsequently and tentatively identified was investigated during diving operations and proved not to be an aircraft. Aviation finds made subsequently during the dredge are provided for in its mitigation protocols.

Recent work in the context of similar dredging schemes elsewhere has also highlighted the potential limitations of the documentary research normally undertaken in the context of marine EIAs (Wessex Archaeology 2011e). Additional documentary research carried out in relation to a proposed scheme in the Bristol Channel has demonstrated that more detailed and comprehensive assessment of documentary sources in areas rich in such sources can produce a significantly different picture of the wrecks and casualties likely to be within a study area than that derived from the standard searches of national and local archaeological records and the UKHO. In particular, it was found that these standard searches underestimate the scale of losses of all periods and that the accuracy of loss location could, in many cases, be greatly improved. In addition, some uncertainties with regard to wreck identification could be resolved.

The extent to which more detailed assessment of documentary evidence available for the dredge channel of the London Gateway scheme could have improved the EIA results, and informed later stages of the archaeological work, is unclear. It is very possible that the overall impact would have been insignificant. However, the Thames Estuary is undoubtedly rich in documentary records and their potential has yet to be fully explored.

The EIA documentation was not monolithic. By March 2003 it had been through an iterative process of refinement, which on the wetside included the addition of further UKHO, NRHE and other wreck and casualty data as a result of changes to the 'red line' extent of the scheme. It also incorporated and integrated the results of geophysical survey undertaken in 2002, adding numerous seabed anomalies and providing additional information concerning the presence, character and extent of previously identified sites.

Further desk-based research was undertaken to inform the preparation of the Clearance Mitigation Statements (CMSs). These were prepared for 29 sites, all known wrecks or obstructions. This phase of research was far more detailed on an individual site level than that undertaken for the EIA, and was guided by the adoption of Wessex Archaeology's Build-Use-Loss-Survival-Investigation (BULSI) model for the investigation of shipwrecks (Wessex Archaeology 2006a). The objectives of the CMSs were to produce a better understanding of the history (both before and after loss) and the importance of the sites, and to thereby inform decisions on what further investigation and mitigation would be required.

Research at this stage centred around the integration of PLA records concerning their involvement on individual sites, including previous clearance and survey work, and more detailed information from the relevant UKHO wreck reports. This work principally informed issues of identification and also the BULSI themes of (post-loss) survival and investigation.

Research was also carried out at the National Archives and at the National Maritime Museum in order to add to knowledge of individual vessel histories and understanding of the build, use and loss themes. The documentation sourced at this stage included ship plans, models and photographs, together with contemporary accounts, investigations, and other documents concerning the actual loss of the vessels concerned.

The research conducted for the CMSs also added considerably to knowledge of one aspect of shipwreck archaeology that has not always received the attention that it deserves – that of the social history of the vessels concerned and their wider place in the history of the Thames Estuary and the people whose lives have revolved around it. The value of this aspect of the investigation was particularly great in respect of the wartime losses, and answered questions of a practical nature such as the potential for the presence of human remains and ordnance. For example, the documentation that survives for requisitioned trawler *Ash*, lost in 1941, provided confirmation that, although ordnance was onboard at the time of loss, no lives were lost and, therefore, human remains were not present on the wreck (see below). In addition, it also provided a level of account of loss that could not have been obtained from archaeological evidence alone, and a more detailed account of the history of the vessel.

The CMSs represented a fairly sophisticated response to the need to draw together in one document all of the available sources of information concerning the wrecks selected for clearance. They provided a clear and consistent method of presenting multiple strands of evidence, and of assessing the importance of each site. They were also largely successful in determining what information was still required from the sites in order to prepare for and mitigate adequately the impact of clearance.

Not all the research was carried out by archaeologists. Professional researchers hired by a TV production company undertook work in relation to a number of wrecks that featured on the subsequent two-part programme *Thames Shipwrecks: a race against time*. In the case of the requisitioned yacht *Aisha* (Site 5057), sunk in 1940 after hitting a mine and subject to geophysical survey during the EIA process, these researchers were particularly successful in obtaining second-hand eye-witness accounts of the sinking from the children of two of the survivors (see below). This level of research went beyond the scope of the scheme itself and represents a flexible and successful synergy of archaeology and media interests.

Marine geophysics

Methods of marine geophysical survey

Geophysical surveys provide a means to rapidly cover a large area in order to remotely sense the properties of the seabed, material lying on it and the geology underlying it. Diver surveys may produce detailed descriptions of a site and recover artefacts but, of necessity, they cover a much smaller area than geophysical surveys and are not suitable for checking for the presence of sites at the scales commonly encountered in development-led archaeology. With the extremely low visibility of the Thames Estuary, among other issues, also making it difficult for divers to survey known sites – especially extensive highly three-dimensional metal vessels – in their entirety, geophysical surveys provide the only means to acquire full coverage ofthe extent of sites whose presence was already known. The value of marine geophysics in 'intrasite' surveying – using geophysical data about the extent, form and character within a site directly in archaeological recording, rather than just presence and position – was one of the methodological advances that accompanied London Gateway. This intensification of the role of geophysics in marine archaeology arose from improvements in instrument resolution, position-fixing, digital recording and the availability to archaeologists of processing software (Firth 2011).

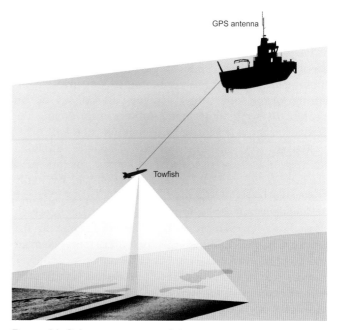

Figure 11: Sidescan sonar towfish

There are several types of marine geophysical survey and many different types of equipment that can be used to acquire data. The four main types were all used on the London Gateway project. These are: sidescan sonar, bathymetric, magnetic and seismic survey.

A *sidescan sonar system* (Fig. 10) measures the intensity and strength of the reflection from the seabed of an acoustic signal it emits. The sidescan sonar towfish is towed below the sea surface on a cable behind a survey vessel. The height of the instrument above the seabed is adjusted by changing the amount of cable out. Transducers on both sides of the towfish emit a narrow, vertical, fan-shaped beam of acoustic energy (Fig. 11). The returning energy is recorded and used to produce acoustic images of the seabed. Upstanding areas of seabed or material reflect back to the towfish a greater proportion of the incident energy from their facing surface than do flat areas of seabed. Similarly, an acoustic shadow is formed behind an upstanding object where acoustic energy does not pass through it. Scours and hollows also appear as shadows or areas of low reflectivity. In addition to the morphology of the seafloor the surface texture of the seabed also effects how much of the acoustic energy is reflected. A rougher seabed produces stronger backscatter and a darker tone on the record (as shown in Part III, below).

Figure 10: Deployment of a sidescan sonar

By using geophysical survey techniques for maritime archaeological purposes, the positions of ship and aircraft wrecks can be mapped and information gained on their dimensions and physical condition. Results are correlated with those of a desk-based assessment to merge available documentary evidence, such as identification, date of loss, and other details, with the current appearance of sites. However, the results of a geophysical survey cannot, on their own, provide information on the archaeological or historical importance of a wreck or other debris.

To detect small objects or low upstanding features the towfish needs to be kept close to the seabed, which emphasises the shadows behind upstanding objects (Fig. 12). The maximum distance (the 'range') over which the signal can pass and still be received by the towfish is reduced the lower the fish altitude is above the seabed.

High resolution sidescan sonar data suitable for archaeological surveys can be acquired using a combination of high frequency acoustics and short-range, typically 500kHz at a range of 50m or 75m.

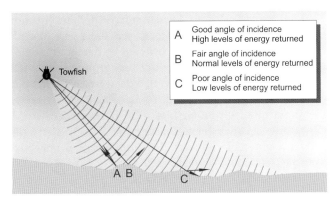

Figure 12: The sidescan sonar produces the best results with the lowest angle of incidence (A)

Bathymetric surveys can be accomplished using either single-beam or multibeam echo sounders. A single-beam echo sounder acquires a series of individual measurements of seabed depth as the survey vessel moves forward. Although once the mainstay of surveying for navigational purposes, especially in ports, the relatively low density of soundings and the need to sail numerous closely-spaced survey lines was leading to much greater use of multibeam echo sounders over the period in which the London Gateway scheme was being prepared. Specifically, multibeam datasets started to be used extensively for archaeological aspects of the scheme from 2005 onwards.

A multibeam echo sounder measures water depth below it with a fan-shaped array of acoustic beams that extend below and to the sides of the survey vessel to acquire a swath of spot depths (hence the alternative term of *swath bathymetry*). The swath width is usually around four times the water depth. The multibeam echo sounder equipment is normally mounted on the hull of a survey vessel, sometimes on a pole over the side rather than directly. As the vessel moves forward continuous and well positioned spot depths are acquired, producing a quantitative record of the seabed bathymetry with its hollows, scours and upstanding objects, from which three-dimensional digital terrain models, site profiles and plans can be created (see for instance Figs 24 and 26, below).

While soundings can be dense enough to show objects on the seabed less than a metre across, multibeam surveys can have difficulty detecting small sites with little vertical expression. Sidescan sonar surveys are better suited for seeking out the presence of small and low-profile features. However, multibeam surveys can quickly map a single site, providing quantitative data to quite a high level of detail. The resolution of the data is dependent on the distance between the sensor and the object: the greater the distance the lesser the resolution. As the Thames is reasonably shallow, the multibeam data provided a relatively high resolution source of information.

Marine magnetometers are used to detect ferrous material lying on or buried below the seabed through

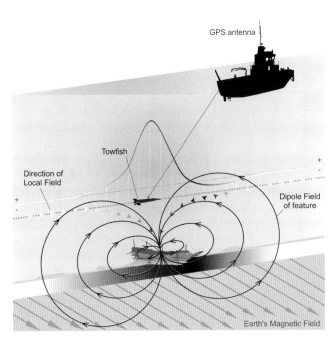

Figure 13: A magnetometer towfish being used to detect a wreck on the seabed

detecting alterations in the strength of the earth's magnetic field (Fig. 13). A magnetometer towfish is towed astern of a survey vessel either individually or 'piggy-backed' off a sidescan sonar towfish by a short cable. In either case the magnetometer must be towed a sufficient distance behind the vessel to avoid picking up any magnetic signal originating from the vessel itself.

Unlike sidescan sonar and multibeam bathymetry data, magnetometer surveys can detect buried material. They can also enable the determination of a wreck as being metal or wooden hulled. In addition, they can be used to detect outlying ferrous material scattered around a wreck site, such as cannon, where the smaller anomalies of these objects are not masked by the large anomalies created by metal wrecks.

Seismic surveys, in contrast to sidescan sonar and bathymetric surveys, are used to 'see' below the seabed rather than to gain information on seabed features. A sound wave is generated that penetrates into the seabed and is partially reflected and refracted at each change in the rock or sediment properties. The reflected signal is recorded and used to map geological and sediment structures below the seabed. As data is obtained from a single line directly under the survey vessel, and the capacity for most seismic systems to 'see' within the top few metres of seabed is quite limited, the data are more commonly used to look for extensive features such as submerged and buried prehistoric landsurfaces rather than wreck sites. However, the *London* (Site 5019/5029) was subject to a seismic survey using a parametric system following its designation under the *Protection of Wrecks Act* 1973, contributing to the understanding of the depth and extent of buried archaeological material associated with the wreck (see below).

London Gateway marine geophysics

Geophysical surveys were undertaken at various stages during the project. Low-resolution sidescan sonar data were acquired in 2001 by Emu Ltd in the course of a boomer (seismic) survey carried out for engineering purposes. A higher resolution sidescan sonar and magnetometer survey with specifically archaeological objectives was carried out by Emu under Wessex Archaeology's supervision in 2002. The data from both 2001 and 2002 were processed by Emu Ltd and Wessex Archaeology. More sophisticated, higher resolution surveys, coupled with diver investigation (see below), were undertaken by the PLA in 2005–7. This improvement in survey quality was partly the product of progressive development in survey equipment over this period but, more specifically it reflected the refinement of survey objectives as the project progressed. The initial surveys covered extensive areas and were used to assess the presence of wrecks and other debris throughout the survey area. The later surveys were detailed, high resolution surveys of individual wreck sites to gain as much information as possible prior to survey by divers and possible clearance.

The first geophysical survey, in 2001 employed sidescan sonar. Data were acquired on two lines along the channel from Shell Haven to approximately Fisherman's Gat, plus three short lines perpendicular to the quay at Shell Haven itself. The lines were 200m apart, at 100m each side of the centre-line of the channel. The total line length was 140km. Data were acquired using an EG&G 272 towfish at 100kHz and with a range of 150m. These parameters were not really optimal for archaeological purposes as they produce low resolution data; however, they did allow for some initial interpretation.

In November 2002 a second geophysical survey was undertaken with data collected according to parameters more suited to archaeological interpretation. Four lines of sidescan sonar and magnetometer data were collected, from Shell Haven along the centre of the shipping channel for 32km to the east, using the same EG&G 272 towfish, but this time a high frequency of approximately 400kHz was used and the range reduced by half to 75m. Magnetic data were acquired using a Geometrics G881 caesium vapour magnetometer.

The sidescan sonar data from both 2001 and 2002 were processed together using Delphmap software. Observed anomalies were subsequently reviewed alongside the results of the earlier desk-based studies. This contributed to the assessment of sites of potential archaeological interest as part of the EIA (see above).

In the course of developing mitigation proposals, the PLA conducted a series of high resolution multibeam surveys, using an 8125 Reson SeaBat system, between late 2005 and the spring of 2006. The data were processed manually by Wessex Archaeology in an extremely detailed fashion in order to pick out as much detail as possible.

The individual data files of ungridded multibeam bathymetry data each contained one short line of data run over an unspecified site, ordered by date and time of acquisition so that they could be grouped by site. Typically, two to eight lines of data were acquired per site, depending on size and any adjacent sites covered by the same lines. Grouped files were converted to PFM (Pure File Magic) format using the IVS Fledermaus software suite to produce a three-dimensional image so that the data could be processed.

The data files contained points labelled as 'rejected'. These tended to be those acquired by the outer beams of the system, which are less accurate, or where a sounding was significantly different in depth to those around it. Where such data points appeared to be part of a wreck or other feature of interest they could be 'un-rejected' and re-included with the good soundings. This tended to happen where objects upstanding or projecting from the main body of a wreck were only 'hit' by a few soundings and it had been assumed that these soundings were incorrect. Conversely, some erroneous points could have been left in the data as they did not differ significantly in depth from surrounding points. Detailed manual processing of the soundings enabled the best possible representation of the wreck or other feature to be produced. Such detailed processing of multibeam data on a sounding by sounding basis is unusual and contributed greatly to the detail of the final surface models.

The data were then gridded with a small cell size of 0.3m in order to provide detailed interpretation of the feature surveyed. The final digital terrain model could then be viewed in Fledermaus and manipulated in three dimensions by tilting and rotating. Measurements and a detailed description of the features in the area could then be made. A geo-referenced map sheet image was exported along with oblique views of the site as tiff images. The geo-referenced image was imported into the project GIS and subsequently used by the divers as a guide if the wreck was subject to diver survey. Both the geo-referenced image and oblique views were included in the CMSs by way of illustration.

For each site covered by bathymetry data the earlier interpretation of the corresponding features in the sidescan sonar data surveys, based on images and descriptions of anomalies considered to have possibly anthropogenic in origin, was assessed. For sites surveyed in 2002, raw data were also available and could be reprocessed and interpreted using Coda Geosurvey software and geo-referenced images of each site produced. These geo-referenced images were included in the CMSs and were also included in the project GIS for use during diver surveys. In addition, where a significant amount of detail of a wreck was seen in the sidescan data it was draped over the multibeam data surface. This enabled direct correlation between the two datasets, further enhancing the interpretation of the wreck.

In July 2007 further multibeam bathymetry data were received from the PLA after a further three wrecks (*Dynamo* (Site 5100), *Erna Boldt* (Site 5961) and

Storm (Site 5960)) had been surveyed. The data were processed following the exacting method described above and images and interpretations were included in the CMSs and made available to the dive team where necessary.

Further sidescan sonar survey was undertaken by the PLA in August 2007, over 13 wrecks for which high resolution multibeam data had already been acquired, processed and interpreted from the earlier surveys. The sidescan data were acquired using an EG&G 272 towfish operating at the high frequency setting of approximately 400kHz. To maximise data resolution the smallest range possible was used: either 50m or 75m depending on the size of the wreck. Geotiff files of each wreck were produced to enable comparison with those from the multibeam data. Further images of the wrecks were also produced in order to show as much detail as possible. The output images were used to update the CMSs for the wrecks and were also to be used for future diving operations. The assessment of this latest geophysical data was used to decide the archaeological mitigation measures to be applied to a number of wreck sites.

Subsequently, the 'King'/*London* sites (Sites 5019/5029) were subject to further geophysical surveys following designation under a separate commission for English Heritage (Wessex Archaeology 2010a).

Diver-based methods

Neither desk-based research of historical records of shipping casualties and salvage and clearance operations, nor geophysical survey data, can currently answer all of the archaeological and heritage management questions posed by schemes such as London Gateway. Geophysical survey is an excellent means of searching for archaeological sites on the seabed and of defining their extent. It is possible to determine whether anomalies have an anthropogenic origin or are natural features, and to start to sort the former into debris and wrecks. Sometimes it is possible to go further and to distinguish between wooden and metal wrecks and other obvious features such as anchors, cables and moorings. However, it is rarely possible to interpret the data much further.

The majority of Wessex Archaeology diving for London Gateway was carried out to characterise features already known to be wrecks rather than to discriminate between anomalies. Discriminating between anomalies by diving inspection would have involved a much larger number of sites to be dived and was not pursued as part of the consenting process.

With the possible exception of the high-resolution survey of very shallow wrecks such as the notorious World War II ammunition shipwreck of the *Richard Montgomery* off Sheerness, diving is currently the only workable, non-intrusive method available to assess the character, date, condition and potential of wreck sites on the seabed in the environmental conditions encountered in the Estuary. Therefore, in order to establish what sites on the seabed actually represent, it is necessary to inspect them physically, by diving.

Archaeological diving investigations were carried out for the London Gateway project after submission of the EIA, during preparation for clearance. As noted above (see also Table 6), diving occurred in two stages, Stages I and II.

Stage I diving was intended to achieve Level 1b (field assessment) and partial 2a (non-intrusive evaluation) site recording during the course of as few as 1–2 dives. It was therefore based largely upon inspection diving with very little or no intrusive work, although finds were recovered from some sites to aid identification and dating.

Stage II diving was intended to achieve an enhanced Level 3 (*in situ* recording). These investigations were intended to be intrusive and the recovery of finds and vessel structure was provided for in the diving objectives.

Underwater inspection can be accomplished by either an ROV or a diver. Although the use of ROVs was contemplated for London Gateway, the relatively shallow water and poor underwater visibility favoured the use of divers. Where depth permits, an archaeologically trained diver generally provides a more flexible and sophisticated means of investigating sites than an ROV, particularly in low visibility environments. In those circumstances, divers – who are inherently more dextrous and have 3D vision, a sense of touch and short-range positional awareness – offer a crucial advantage over ROV.

Diving was carried out by two types of team: a stand-alone Wessex Archaeology team and a PLA dive team which included 'embedded' Wessex Archaeology or other specialist divers. In the former case Wessex Archaeology operated in November 2007 as the diving contractor with a team of up to six permanent and contracted staff, deployed aboard a chartered dive support vessel. Wessex Archaeology provided all of the diving and archaeological equipment. As the diving and archaeological contractor, Wessex Archaeology was responsible for all aspects of the operation, with the exception that responsibility for positioning the dive support vehicle on each site investigated was devolved to the vessel operators.

In the case of embedded diving, apart from one operation comprising three dives in 2005 involving Nigel Nayling (University of Wales Trinity Saint David), either one or two Wessex Archaeology divers were embedded as part of the PLA's own permanent dive team. The PLA was the diving contractor and provided their small dedicated dive support vehicle, *PLA Diver*, together with the basic diving equipment. The PLA team were responsible for getting the divers to the site and for the safe conduct of diving operations. The embedded Wessex Archaeology divers undertook the bulk of the diving and were responsible for the conduct of the archaeological work. The PLA divers undertook some of the inspection and recovery work but key tasks were generally carried out by archaeologists.

Figure 14: Diver wearing surface supply equipment preparing to dive

In addition, some information was derived from the results of PLA-only diving operations on a number of sites. These were independent operations and were not undertaken as part of the Stage I or II diving programme.

Generally speaking, Wessex Archaeology provided all of the archaeological equipment. For the most part, finds were recovered to the surface by hand. However, intrusive investigation and the recovery of vessel structure were anticipated during Stage II work on Sites 5051 and 5204. For this the PLA supplied one of their dedicated salvage vessels, the *Hookness*, for work on these sites. This vessel was fitted with winches for lifting and also a large crane-deployed airlift.

Some difficulty was experienced with the dive support vessel during the stand-alone Wessex Archaeology diving operation. Concerns with regard to the distance between shore bases and some of the sites and the long transit times that would ensue, and with the need for a substantial presence in the busy waterway, meant that this operation was designed from the outset to be based on a fairly large vessel that would remain at sea with the dive team on board. The need to securely anchor the vessel on-site presented a challenge, however this issue was exacerbated by the season in which the work was commissioned and the worst storm surge in the Thames for 20 years.

In contrast, Wessex Archaeology embedded diving proceeded more smoothly. Employing the PLA to provide diving support also enabled the archaeologists to take advantage of their diving team's local knowledge with regard to the timing and duration of diveable slack-water periods. It is a model that Wessex Archaeology had used successfully elsewhere, in investigations in Wexford, the Shannon and Belfast Lough in the late 1990s for example. Whilst it is unlikely to have universal application because a suitably experienced local team may not be available, combined teams of commercial and archaeological divers are likely to have application to many areas of development-led archaeology.

Industry standard surface supplied diving equipment was used during all diving operations (Fig. 14). The relative efficacy of surface supplied and SCUBA (self-contained underwater breathing apparatus) diving techniques for archaeology has been the subject of some debate in the UK in recent years. However, in the case of London Gateway, the question of which technique to use did not arise. Divers at work in the UK are highly regulated and SCUBA is only regarded as suitable for use by working divers in reasonably benign environments. As all of the sites were in difficult and potentially hazardous diving environments, SCUBA was discounted from the outset. This decision also facilitated the involvement of the PLA dive team, which uses surface supply.

As with SCUBA, surface supplied divers work in a team, part of which remains on the surface. The size of the team is normally determined on the basis of job safety and to comply with UK diving regulations. Beyond that it is determined by the objectives and budget available. For most of the London Gateway diving operations a team of five was available, one more than the regulatory minimum. The additional person was required to operate the archaeological recording and acoustic positioning system, discussed below.

A surface supplied diver receives an air supply from the surface, whilst also carrying a small supply sufficient for emergency use. He or she works alone on the seabed, wearing a helmet that provides a comfortable working environment. Two-way voice communications, a powerful helmet-mounted light and a helmet-mounted camera, whose video feed is displayed on a surface monitor, enabling dive team members and other specialists on the surface to participate in archaeological recording, as well as facilitating the use of an acoustic positioning system (Fig. 15).

The dive is controlled from the surface by the dive supervisor. He or she controls the diver's air supply and runs the safety aspects of the dive, informing the diver when to dive and when to return to the surface, as well as assisting diver navigation. A second diver, who is in immediate readiness to enter the water, remains on the surface as a 'stand-by' (rescue) diver. A non-diving tender manages the 'umbilical' of hoses and cables that connect the diver to the surface and operates plant on deck. As a result, the diver is left to concentrate on the work in hand and is not overloaded with safety-critical tasks.

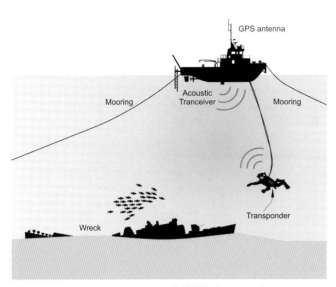

Figure 15: Ultra Short Baseline (USBL) diver tracking system

In some circumstances the stand-by can work with the diver on the seabed. However, both divers must be able to reach the other very quickly in the event of an emergency, which normally means that they must work within sight of each other and maintain a close awareness of the status of the other. This restricts the ability of both divers to work independently and reduces their individual efficiency. In the case of London Gateway sites, the very poor visibility would have required the divers to have worked within touching distance and they would have inevitably obstructed each other. Alternatively, operations could have been carried out using two divers independently, but would have required an additional tender and stand-by on the surface, increasing the cost and complexity of operations constrained by tide and underwater visibility. Consequently, all diving operations were conducted by a single diver in the water.

Inspection by non-archaeological PLA divers proved to be effective in determining whether anthropogenic material was present and in helping to establish the extent of sites. Whilst some information about the character of the sites investigated was certainly produced, non-archaeological divers were less successful in terms of the volume and quality of the archaeologically useful information generated. This is likely to have been due to the limited scope of the work that they undertook as well as lack of specialist archaeological knowledge. As a result, investigation by PLA divers generally had to be treated as preliminary and followed up by archaeological diver investigation.

An example of this occurred on Site 5019, at the time known as the 'King' site but now known to contain wreck material from both the 17th-century warship London and from an unidentified 19th- or early 20th-century wreck (see below). Investigation by a non-archaeological diver reported it as a wooden wreck, but failed to distinguish it from the much earlier wreck material immediately to the north, and so provided a potentially misleading description of its structural form.

Subsequent inspection by a Wessex Archaeology diver enabled its structural form to be identified and distinguished from the earlier wreck, and for a post-1840 date to be established.

Archaeological methodology underwater depends to a great extent upon the ability of a diver to both identify an object whilst on the seabed and to determine its relationship to other nearby objects. Both these interpretative processes interact and, in the absence of contextual information, it is often difficult to identify objects which are partly buried or whose form may have been modified by complex interaction with the environment over a long period of time. Archaeologists tend to rely on visual inspection in order to accomplish both tasks. Indeed, to some extent, this may have conditioned where archaeological diving investigations have taken place in the past.

In addition, in the past much underwater archaeology has been undertaken by volunteer divers who have tended to investigate sites in areas where they have already been diving recreationally, which are less likely to be those with very poor visibility. As a result, methodology and training have tended to assume that even if visibility is quite low – perhaps down to 0.5–1.0m – it will normally be adequate.

Archaeologists working in development-led archaeology on projects such as London Gateway do not choose the environment in which they dive. Many of those environments are subject to very poor underwater visibility. For example, in the immediate environs of ports and harbours subject to redevelopment, in port approaches subject to dredging and, to a lesser extent, offshore in areas subject to renewable energy or aggregate dredging schemes, no effective visibility ('black water' or 'nil-visibility'), or visibility significantly less than 1m is frequently encountered. As a result, archaeologists working in the development-led sector have had to develop methodologies for recording and interpreting sites underwater that can cope with nil-visibility.

Although methodological issues encountered during archaeological projects underwater tend not to be routinely discussed in any detail in the resulting publications, there have been occasional exceptions. For example, simple methods to deal with the lack of visibility such as the use of clear water 'visibility bags' were developed for the recording of the paddle steamer Maple Leaf in the dark environment of the St John's River in North Florida by East Carolina University (Van Tilburg 1994). However, no low cost 'perfect solution' has been developed that is capable of easy and rapid deployment. Furthermore, it is clear from the work on the Maple Leaf and others that the solutions that have been devised tend to rely upon considerable time being available both on-site and for training, a circumstance that is not generally available to archaeologists undertaking development-led contracts in the UK.

Underwater visibility in the Thames Estuary is generally very poor, as the water column contains a large quantity of particulate matter. This is generally silt and other fine grained sediment that has a predominantly riverine origin, although fine grained sediment brought into the estuary from the southern North Sea, and seasonal algal bloom and similar natural phenomena, can be factors too. Experience during London Gateway and other projects has demonstrated that visibility tends to worsen to the west as the influence of the river increases and to improve, slightly, towards the east as the influence of the sea increases. That influence is tidal and the presence of water brought in from the open sea by a flood tide tends to produce slightly better visibility on a site than that produced on the ebb. Sea state is also a factor and settled weather can produce slightly better visibility. These factors combine to ensure that although, under exceptional conditions, visibility of 2–3m can be encountered, visibility exceeding 1m is rare and the norm is 0.5m or less.

Even visibility of 0.5m does not, of course, mean that everything within that distance can be seen clearly. On all of the sites investigated during the project, the existence of any visibility at all depended upon the availability of artificial light. A number of sites investigated by Wessex Archaeology divers as part of embedded teams were investigated without any effective visibility because artificial light was not available.

When artificial light was available, its use was complicated because it inevitably illuminates the particulate matter in the water column between the light source and the object being examined. This means that, although an object that is 1m away from the light source may be illuminated, it may only be seen as an indistinct outline and detail may not be apparent even close up. Furthermore, tapes and compasses become very difficult or impossible to read, rendering traditional survey methods ineffective. The best solution found was to use a hand-held rather than helmet-mounted light source. Although this still produced poor illumination, the archaeological divers involved in the project generally felt that the use of a light source, however dim, was always a significant advantage.

Experience on the project demonstrated that the combination of light source and examination by touch often enabled the archaeologist to identify the form and function of an individual object. If that object was partly buried or eroded, or part of a larger composite or otherwise complex object, then identification was less likely. Lack of any light source made identification more problematic and less reliable, unless the form of the object was so distinct that it could not be misidentified, for example the tool handles found on Site 5051 (see below).

However, the availability of a light source did not resolve the problem of understanding the relationship between an individual object and its surroundings. Generally speaking the relationship between objects could only be determined if they were next to each other. The greater the distance apart they were, the greater was the difficulty in resolving their relationship. This was compounded by the difficulty experienced in diver navigation and orientation. Divers who do not have effective visibility have greatly reduced situational

awareness and, if they are unable to read a compass, then they may not even know which direction they are facing. Locating and relocating objects on the seabed, for example geophysical anomalies, then becomes extremely difficult.

Diving investigations undertaken for the scheme in 2005 are a good example of the impact that this can have on archaeological results. These investigations were undertaken without a light source in nil-visibility conditions. Although an archaeological diver was able to give a coherent description of individual features encountered during a dive on Site 5019 (part of the *London* wreck), it remains unclear as to where within the site these features were found. The resulting uncertainty with regard to the position of a large bronze gun found during that dive, relative to archaeological features found during more recent diving investigations, has made it impossible to determine whether it was one of the cannon salvaged in 2007 and, therefore, whether or not it remains on the seabed. In addition, no form of spatial plan of the archaeological features was achieved and it has not proved possible to reconcile the diver observations fully with available geophysical data.

During most of the archaeological diving investigations, the potential difficulties imposed by the lack of visibility were partially overcome using an acoustic positioning system. This greatly improved diver navigation, enabling geophysical anomalies to be reliably located on the seabed. It also provided what was often the only means of establishing the spatial relationship between individual archaeological features, and of mapping the sites concerned.

The system used was a Sonardyne Scout Ultra Short Baseline (USBL) acoustic positioning system, the application of which to archaeology has been developed by Wessex Archaeology in the context of development-led work and research projects such as ALSF *Wrecks on the Seabed* (Wessex Archaeology 2004). USBL systems (sometimes called Super Short Baseline or SSBL) calculate the position of a sub-sea target such as a diver by measuring the range and bearing using acoustic signals from a vessel-mounted transceiver to a small acoustic transponder fitted to the diver. 'Real world' positions for the transponder are then calculated by the system using data from a vessel mounted Differential Global Positioning System (dGPS). Figure 15 shows a typical system set-up. In addition to tracking divers, USBL systems are widely used offshore to track ROVs and instruments, and to position other sub-sea equipment and structures. However, the routine use of acoustic positioning systems by archaeologists is subject to cost, familiarity and training issues. It is difficult to use without reliable voice communications between the diver and the surface and it requires a level of investment both financially and in expertise that is not always available to archaeological teams.

The calculation of range and bearing by a USBL system depends upon two principles. The first is that an accurate range can be determined by knowing precisely the time taken for the acoustic signal to travel between the transponder and the transceiver, and the speed of the signal (the speed of sound in the water column). The second is that the bearing can be calculated by knowing the discrete difference in phase between the receipt of the signal at the multiple transducers fitted in the transceiver; this allows the system to determine a time-phase difference for each transducer and to calculate the angle of the arriving acoustic signal.

As well as an acoustic transceiver and a transponder, the Scout system also has attitude sensors for the accurate determination of vessel pitch, roll and heading. The data produced by these instruments enable vessel and, therefore, transceiver movement to be accommodated without loss of accuracy.

In this instance the transponder was attached to the diver's umbilical just above the diver, rather than to the diver, to ensure that line of sight between the transponder and the transceiver would not be blocked by the diver's body. Mounting the transponder to a hand-held pole was considered but rejected on the grounds that it would be too cumbersome in the conditions likely to be encountered.

The position of the transponder and, therefore, of the diver were then exported to DIVA, a Microsoft Access database recording system developed by Wessex Archaeology operated by an archaeologist on the diving support vessel. DIVA records archaeological and environmental data as observation points that are linked to the position provided by the acoustic system (Firth 2011).

DIVA offers a number of distinct advantages over traditional in-water recording systems, which proved to be critical in the poor visibility environment experienced during the project. First, it does not depend on the diver's ability to write or draw while on the seabed, a slow and potentially impracticable task in poor visibility. Secondly, it enables multiple sources of data, including acoustic positioning, video, and descriptions and measurements verbally communicated to the diver, as well as the observations of colleagues on the surface, to be recorded in real time. Thirdly, DIVA has a GIS interface that enables the position and track of the diver to be displayed in relation to previous observation points and in relation to geophysical survey data, such as georeferenced sidescan sonar or bathymetric images (Fig. 16). This enables the diver to be navigated from the surface (even in nil-visibility), geophysical anomalies to be reliably located, evaluation trenches and test pits to be recorded, and areas that have been searched to be defined accurately. It provides an additional safety factor in that the position of the diver in relation to the diving support vessel is always known, and it also enables the vessel to be accurately positioned over the site before diving commences. This minimises the time taken by the diver to travel to the site, increasing the proportion of dive time devoted to actual archaeological investigation.

A further advantage of the DIVA recording system is that it is observation-based rather than object-based. Most conventional archaeological recording systems are based on 'things' such as contexts, features, timbers,

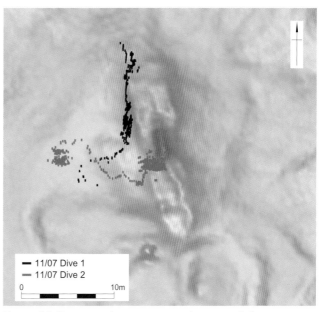

Figure 16: Diver track superimposed on a multibeam image of a shipwreck

artefacts and so on, and assume that the basic attributes of these things can be recorded immediately and without difficulty. In contrast, DIVA is designed to record observations as a series of small events in the course of a dive. This means that DIVA is better able to cope with the highly contingent qualities of underwater observations in difficult environments, which can accrue and be reconsidered iteratively. DIVA preserves all the real-time observations made over many dives, meaning that the 'facts' about a site can be arrived at transparently and can be readily reconsidered in the light of new data.

Perhaps the most important feature of the DIVA recording system for the type of work undertaken is that it enables very rapid surveys of sites to be carried out. This is a particular advantage when, as during the London Gateway project, time on site was severely limited by the environment, and by the constraints imposed by budgets and timetables. For most of the daily tidal cycle, the currents are simply too strong for a diver to work safely on the seabed. Diving is limited to short slack-water periods that occur in approximate relationship to low water and high water. The timing and length of these slack-water periods vary but they were found to only rarely exceed one hour. For a single shift diving team that might be able to dive once or twice per day, and taking into account travel time between the vessel and the site, daily working time on site rarely exceeded two hours and was often significantly less.

This lack of time on site placed a premium on the efficient recording practices, something that traditional archaeological methodology underwater, with its reliance upon laborious tape measurements, diver sketches and written descriptions compiled on-site, does not usually provide. DIVA, when combined with acoustic positioning, provided a solution that enabled a dive team led by a diver on the seabed to record sites during just one or two dives.

The excavation and recovery methods used in the context of Stage II diving operations must also be understood in terms of the very difficult environmental conditions and the severe time constraints that they imposed on the work. The time available on sites investigated was very limited and Level 3 recording could not always be achieved because of this constraint. As stated elsewhere the scheme often required investigation to be rapid. The slow and methodical excavation carried out on relatively benign UK shipwreck sites, such as the *Colossus* in the Scillies, the Swash Channel site off Poole and, in particular, on the 17th-century wreck at Duart Point in Scotland (Martin 1995) or, for example, in response to dredging in the Arade River in Portugal by Filipe Castro and others (Castro 2005) was simply not an option.

A large crane-deployed airlift was used to excavate, together with a lifting winch to recover vessel structure. The former proved to be particularly advantageous for Site 5051 due to the substantial volume of sediment encountered lying over the deposits of archaeological interest. The limited time available on site, the large size and limited manoeuvrability of the airlift and the very difficult in-water recording conditions meant that detailed recording could not be achieved underwater. Therefore, provision was made for vessel structure to be recorded after recovery in a manner similar to that adopted for the Gresham Ship (Auer and Firth 2007) and for the outwash of the airlift to empty and be sorted on deck.

Although the excavation and recovery methods used were certainly not delicate, they provided an effective means of exposing and recovering material from both sites in the time available. They enabled vessel structure to be recovered from Site 5204 that identified the type of vessel and its probable date range, although time limitations meant that the vessel structure encountered could not be lifted whole or completely. Whilst Site 5051 proved to be too large and too deeply buried for vessel structure to be recovered, finds were recovered from the outwash and by the diver that allowed the broad type and date of the vessel to be established with reasonable confidence.

In terms of the diving the challenging environment and the need to comply with UK diving regulations meant that low cost solutions were unsuitable. Whilst appreciation and comparison is limited by the relative lack of discussion of methodology in many archaeological site reports, there does seem to have been little in the existing archaeological experience that was readily transferable. As a result more cost-effective methods of rapid diver investigation developed in the context of previous development-led diving investigations and ALSF research were applied. As this research was on-going during the London Gateway project there was therefore a useful interchange of experience. Overall, the diving methods proved to be well suited to the needs of the scheme and may inform development-led investigations in the UK and abroad in future. However, and as will be seen in Part III, success on an individual site level was ultimately measured by the scale of resources applied.

Maritime Archaeology in the Thames – the Contribution of London Gateway

INTRODUCTION

This volume does not discuss medieval and earlier periods. This is simply because the investigations conducted did not lead to the 'wetside' discovery of archaeological evidence predating the post-medieval period. This is disappointing but not surprising. Such evidence, if it occurs, tends to be physically quite ephemeral and therefore hard to detect. Furthermore, the scheme is largely based upon an existing modern shipping channel. Whilst later wrecks would be expected in and around this channel, no such clustering would be expected from smaller medieval and earlier vessels as they would not have been constrained or channelled by it.

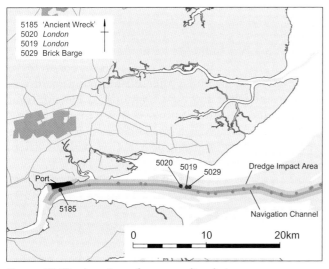

Figure 17: The location of post-medieval sites

Archaeological investigation of post-medieval subtidal wrecks in the Thames Estuary has been very limited and where investigations have occurred they have tended to focus on intertidal or 'dryside' locations (Essex County Council 2010, 27). Shell Haven was used as a port from the 16th century and three of the sites investigated for London Gateway have been dated to the post-medieval period (Fig. 17).

Thematic approaches to the study of groups of wreck sites have been gaining ground in the UK in recent years. For example, the desk-based and geophysical assessments of wrecks associated with the Welsh coal and slate industries commissioned by Cadw are now for the first time leading to a full appreciation of the potential importance of wreck sites to the study of those industries (Wessex Archaeology 2009a–b and 2010b). This approach provides a strong contextual background to the study of wreck sites, as well as promoting a more integrated approach to wet and dryside archaeology.

The discussion below therefore approaches the wrecks investigated using two themes of vital importance to the proper understanding of the history of the Estuary in this period: maritime trade and commerce and naval warfare and maritime defence. It also examines the contribution that the investigation of these three sites has made to post-medieval archaeology generally and to the evolution of marine archaeological methods.

It is worth noting that investigation for London Gateway of these three sites (and the others discussed below) has been relevant to and has directly influenced the latest regional archaeological research agenda, *The Greater Thames Estuary Historic Environment Research Framework* 2010 (Essex County Council 2010). This document is an updated version of the research framework issued by Essex County Council in 1999. This recognised the key framework objective of maritime archaeology in the Greater Thames Estuary:

> 'to examine the role of the estuary in providing internal coherence through trading and other maritime contacts and as a major artery of communication between England and continental Europe' (Williams and Brown 1999, 29).

This remains the key framework objective. In synthesising the available data on a large number of wreck sites, in developing a clear protocol for selecting and recording vessel remains and in facilitating systematic record enhancement of a very important maritime highway within the estuary, the London Gateway project has progressed, and to a large extent anticipated, current archaeological strategy (Essex County Council 2010, 30).

Maritime trade and commerce

During the 16th and 17th centuries the maritime trade of London and the Thames Estuary grew steadily until about nine-tenths of the country's commerce passed through the port of London. During the 18th century the volume of maritime traffic passing through the Thames Estuary grew dramatically, fuelled by agricultural and industrial revolutions, the expansion of Britain's overseas interests, the growth of the canal network and the demands of the capital's growing population.

Most of this traffic was destined for or travelling from London, which was rapidly becoming the greatest port in the world. By the end of the century trade had reached such levels that the city was struggling to cope with the number of ships arriving and departing and massive new dock schemes had started to be developed. Despite the growth of regional ports, by the end of the period London was still handling about a third of the vessels entering or clearing English and Welsh ports (Jackson 1983, 31).

Archaeological evidence of the wrecks associated with this trade in the Thames is fairly sparse. Key examples include the 16th-century 'Gresham Ship' from the Princes Channel (Auer and Firth 2007, 232) (Figs 3–4) and the post-medieval vessels (Blackfriars II and Blackfriars IV) recovered during excavations of a 16th-century waterfront in Southwark in 1987 (Marsden 1996, 144, 153). Two of the three post-medieval sites investigated for London Gateway have been identified as associated with this theme.

Site 5020 ('Iron Bar Wreck')

(W of Sea Reach 4, *c* 5.5km off Southend-on-Sea; depth 12.7m, Figs 17, 18)

Site 5020 was first located during periodic survey in 1978 and was partly salvaged by the PLA later that same year. It was described as an 'old vessel' and as the wreck of an unknown wooden vessel containing a cargo of iron bars. It was only partially cleared because signs of debris were observed during a survey the following year. However, by 1985 the wreck seems to have become buried, as detailed soundings failed to find it.

The site was identified in both the 2001 and 2002 London Gateway sidescan sonar surveys and during PLA multibeam surveys in 2004 and 2006 with an area of possible wreck debris and an outlying scour observed (Fig. 18). The site was dived in February 2005 by the PLA (with Nigel Nayling).

Although further diving investigation was proposed prior to clearance, the archaeological sensitivity prompted changes to the design of the channel to avoid the site. The same mitigation strategy was also applied to Site 5019/5029 the *London* (ultimately designated under the *Protection of Wrecks Act* 1973).

No further investigation was carried out although the site has been monitored during subsequent geophysical survey.

In 2005, Nigel Nayling reported a debris field consisting of numerous folded iron bars, including a large concreted mass, together with fragments of oak vessel frames with wooden treenails (Nayling 2005a, 4–5). In addition, 'a significant number' of handmade bricks were found, although none of these appear to have been recovered and it remains unclear whether these were cargo or part of the vessel's galley hearth (PLA 2005a). A sample of the timber framing and a section of concreted rope were recovered for identification. The subsequent PLA multibeam survey in 2006 indicated that the site consisted of a low mound about 7m square within a larger less well defined raised anomaly.

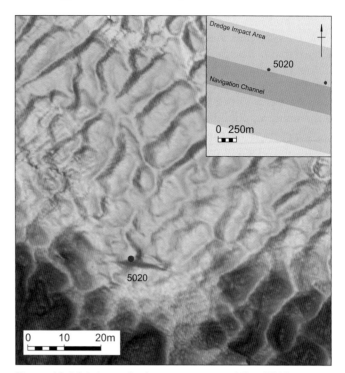

Figure 18: Multibeam bathymetry image of Site 5020 'Iron Bar Wreck'

The discovery of timber frames means that we can be confident that it is the remains of a vessel, but we have little evidence concerning when it was built, what it was used for and when and how it was lost. It has not been linked to the documented loss of a vessel and the fate of the material salvaged in 1978 is unknown, with unrecorded disposal being the overwhelmingly likely outcome. The recovered timber frame was small with a pronounced curve and might indicate that the vessel was small in size, although the observed geophysical anomaly is fairly large.

It has not yet been possible to date the remains. Successfully selecting samples for dendrochronological analysis in zero visibility is highly problematic and the fragment of oak frame recovered in 2005 was unfortunately not suitable for dating. The treenails and oak framing suggest, but do not prove, a pre-20th century date.

Folded or unfolded iron bars have been found as cargo on a number of post-medieval wrecks in the UK, including the 16th-century Gresham wreck, (Auer and Firth 2007, 232–3), the 1743 Dutch VOC loss *Hollandia* in the Scilly Isles (Gawronski *et al.* 1992), the 17th- or 18th-century wreck at West Bay, Dorset (Wessex Archaeology 2006c, 4) and on 19th-century East Indiamen such as the *Hindostan*, lost in the Outer Thames Estuary in 1803 (Redknapp 1990, 27; Wessex Archaeology forthcoming). Earlier evidence for the coastal trade in iron is also known, such as the mid-13th-century Magor Pill wreck with a cargo of iron ore (Nayling 1998). Organised fleets associated with the iron trade are recorded in documentary evidence from as early as the 12th century (Murphy 2009, 79).

The presence of the iron bars indicates that this was a merchant vessel and the position of the wreck may suggest that it was travelling to or from a harbour upriver of the mouth of the Medway. Iron was certainly in growing demand for industry throughout the post-medieval period in London and its hinterland, as well as in the many shipbuilding ports of the Lower Thames.

Whilst the work carried out for the London Gateway scheme in respect of Site 5020 has raised more questions than it has answered, the investigation has led to the recognition of a potentially significant site, a wreck which although it was known had escaped the attention of archaeologists. The site has the potential to inform our knowledge of the coastal iron trade and the early industrial use of the metal in the region and beyond. Until more extensive diving investigation is undertaken, the site's true potential is unlikely to be realised. However, the input of archaeologists at an early stage, and the use of geophysical survey to indicate the extent of survival, has resulted in a wreck being safeguarded that is otherwise likely to have been dispersed during clearance.

Site 5185 ('Ancient Wreck')

(200m NE of the West Blyth Buoy, off the London Gateway port; depth 10.4m, Fig. 17)

This site is the reported position of a 'wooden craft' or 'ancient wooden vessel' that was grabbed clear to bed level by the PLA in 1968 (PLA 2005b). The site was subject to sidescan survey in 2001 and 2002 for London Gateway when a 'cable-like' anomaly was detected. Subsequent multibeam surveys failed to detect the site in 2005 and 2006, although an unidentified anomaly was detected 100m to the east and could be associated, as the original position for the cleared wreck was of uncertain accuracy.

In 2007 the site was resurveyed using sidescan sonar and subject to diving investigation including systematic probing. No archaeological features or artefacts were observed.

The 'Ancient Wreck' was originally considered to be of probable archaeological interest. However, the lack of any evidence for archaeological remains at this location suggested that either the original reported position was wrong or that the wreckage left below bed level during the clearance work in 1968 had become buried. Following the diving investigation, the anomalies seen in the geophysical data to the east were subsequently reinterpreted as natural features.

The record of an ancient wreck at this location remains enigmatic; repeated investigation of the area using a variety of techniques provided confidence that there was no wreck in the immediate vicinity, but the true character of what was cleared in 1968 remains unknown.

The mid-17th-century wreck of the London

For much of the second half of the 17th century, English foreign policy was dominated by a series of trade wars that were fought with the Dutch. These were essentially maritime conflicts, fought mainly in the English Channel and the southern North Sea. It therefore became essential to base the English navy in the South East. Fleet anchorages at the Nore in the Thames Estuary and in the Downs off the east coast of Kent were supported by royal dockyards in the River Thames and Medway, the most important of which was at Chatham. These dockyards provided shipbuilding and repair facilities, stores and a safe haven to over-winter the ships of the fleet.

Naval shipbuilding programmes were undertaken in response to a range of specific threats, including those from Spain during the reign of Elizabeth I, the actions of Barbary corsairs during the reign of Charles I, and the isolation of the Commonwealth of England during the interregnum following the Civil War (Rodger 1997, 379–94). The Commonwealth period (1649–1660) in particular saw great expansion in shipbuilding, the need for new vessels being particularly urgent before and after the First Anglo-Dutch War (1652–4; Fox 1980).

Within the Thames Region, previous archaeological research has addressed the naval dockyards and other dryside sites, for example the 18th-century naval facilities at Woolwich in 2004 (Goodburn *et al.* 2011, 306–27). In contrast to the wider South East region the Estuary has yielded little wreck-based evidence of this period of naval expansion and conflict, and of the naval society that developed from it.

The investigation of two sites for London Gateway has led to a recognition that the Thames Estuary contains one of the most important post-medieval naval wrecks in the UK.

Sites 5019 and 5029: the wreck of the London

(Vicinity of Sea Reach 4, *c* 6km from Southend-on-Sea; depth 11–12.5m, Figs 17, 19)

In the early 1960s (probably 1961), the PLA's Wreck Raising Service under Captain G. R. Rees investigated an echo-sounder contact on the north side of the Yantlet Channel between Sea Reach 4 and 5. The diver sent down on what is thought to have been Site 5019 observed "a lot of timber ribs of an old wooden ship" and followed what appears to have been the hull of a vessel for about 30m. The following day the site was wire swept and a 17th-century bronze cannon was recovered and subsequently accessioned by the Royal Armouries.

Recorded hydrographic data indicates that the site suffered a loss of up to 2m of deposits between 1973 and 1979 but the cause of this is uncertain (Wessex Archaeology 2011f, 22–3). By 1979 the site was reportedly degrading, presumably as a result of this exposure.

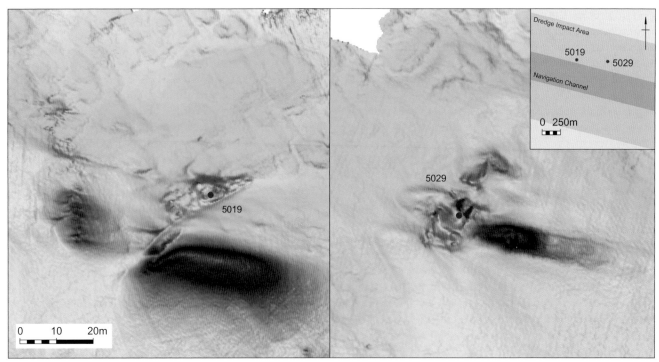

Figure 19: Multibeam bathymetry images of Sites 5019 and 5029, the *London*

Site 5019 was apparent in the 2001 and 2002 geophysical surveys for London Gateway and was targeted by multibeam survey in 2006. The site was also subject to diving investigation by the PLA with Nigel Nayling in January 2005. Further diving investigations were carried out at the site by the PLA with Wessex Archaeology in October 2007 following reports of unauthorised salvage of cannon from the site earlier in the year (Fig. 6).

The 2005 diving investigation was conducted in zero visibility with no artificial light and there were subsequent problems with identifying the position of the diver when observations were made. The archaeological diver understandably admits that he did not know where he was during the dive (Nigel Nayling, pers. comm.). Consequently, the results are confusing because it is not clear from the diver descriptions where the archaeological features observed were. The use of diver tracking systems during subsequent dives has substantially resolved this issue with greater positional accuracy allowing a more detailed understanding of nature and extent of the wreckage.

Site 5029 was discovered in late 1979, approximately 400m east of 5019 as 'an unusual looking feature' in a PLA hydrographic survey. Acting on that discovery, PLA divers salvaged the site in 1980, recovering two cannon whose subsequent disposition is unknown. In 1985 the Royal Navy, acting at the request of the Chatham Historic Dockyard deployed the minesweeper HMS Sheraton to survey the site. There is some indication that a number of cannon-like anomalies were detected but differing views as to the likelihood of individual bronze cannon being detected by the survey equipment in use have been expressed to Wessex Archaeology by mine warfare officers, past and present. Unfortunately any data recorded does not appear to have been retained.

Available hydrographic records suggest that whereas a wreck mound of over 3m may have existed in 1985, erosion over the next 20 years may have removed up to 2m from this mound (Wessex Archaeology 2011f, 11).

Although Site 5029 was identified at an early stage as being of archaeological significance by the scheme, it lay outside the footprint of the 2001 and 2002 geophysical survey area, though a low-resolution sidescan image was provided by the PLA. Site 5029 was surveyed in 2004 when three distinct bathymetric anomalies were found within an area of about 24m by 15m (PLA 2005d; Fig. 19). The site, along with 5019, was also dived by the PLA with Nigel Nayling in 2005. In 2007 sidescan survey was carried out at the site and the site was dived by Wessex Archaeology in 2008.

Sites 5019 and 5029 were both assessed as having certain archaeological interest in the course of the EIA on the basis of the discoveries recorded from the early 1960s and 1980, and the confirmed presence of significant sidescan anomalies at both sites. The relation between the 'King' and the *London* was, however, unclear; though it certainly seemed possible that the 'King' was also a contender for being the *London* because of the date of the bronze cannon found in the early 1960s (see above). This might have meant that Site 5029, although known as the London, might prove to be an altogether different ship.

In response to the vulnerability that the unauthorised salvage in 2007 clearly demonstrated, the *London* was designated under the *Protection of Wrecks Act* (1973) in 2008. Both 5019 and 5029 were included in the single designation as separate designated areas on the basis that both were likely to contain part of the wreck of the *London*. Although neither site had produced archaeological evidence that meant that the material present could come from no other wreck than the *London*, the evidence accumulated during the investigations for the scheme was nevertheless persuasive.

As with Site 5020, the 'Iron Bar Wreck', the sensitivity of Sites 5019 and 5029 was such that changes were made to the design of the London Gateway channel to avoid the sites.

'This morning is brought to me to the office the sad news of the *London*, in which Sir J Lawsons men were all bringing her from Chatham to the Hope, and thence he was to go to sea in her – but a little a-this-side the buoy of the Nower, she suddenly blew up. About 24 and a woman that were in the round house and coach saved; the rest, being 300, drowned – the ship breaking all in pieces – with 80 pieces of brass ordinance. She lies sunk, with her round house above water. Sir J. Lawson hath a great loss in this, of so many chosen men, and many relations among them.'

So wrote the famous diarist and naval administrator Samuel Pepys the day after the loss of Charles II's warship *London* on 7 March 1665. Ever the administrator with a keen eye for money, Pepys would have been concerned about the cannon as well as the men, which would have cost at least as much as the ship to replace.

The *London* was an important Second Rate warship built in Chatham for the Commonwealth government in 1654–6. Flush-decked, 37m long and 12.5m in the beam, it carried a mixed armament of 64 cannon when launched and is representative of a period in which the design of major warships was evolving (Fig. 20). Described as 'a lusty ship' by a contemporary newspaper (*Mercurius Politicus* 1656), it served the Commonwealth before becoming part of Charles II's restored Royal Navy. The ship was part of the squadron that transported Charles back to England for his restoration in 1660 and carried his brother, James Duke of York and his entourage. However, on 7 March 1665, as it sailed out of the Medway with 76 guns on board to collect its Admiral from the Hope at the start of the Second Dutch War, the *London* met the fate described by Pepys.

The gun recovered from Site 5019 in 1960 was cast in Le Havre in 1636, is now in the collection of the Royal Armouries. Although it is French, it is incised with its weight in the English manner and was probably captured by the Commonwealth navy in 1652–4 (Fox 2012, 59; Blackmore 1976, 115). By 1979 the site seems to have become known to the PLA as the 'King', although why this was so remains unclear, unless it refers to the crowned initial of Louise XIII on the recovered gun. It is reported to have been charted as 'K' (PLA 2005c). Unfortunately, a description of two cannon salvaged from Site 5029 in 1980 has not been traced and their fate is unknown.

On Site 5029, geophysical survey had shown the remains in three distinct sections. During the 2005 diving, the northern anomaly was found to consist of a disturbed concentration of ship's timbers including both planking and framing. Modern intrusions, possibly from attempted earlier clearance, salvage or fishing operations were also observed. The central anomaly was the largest and most coherent section of wreckage. Thick timber

Figure 20: Portrait of the *London* by Willem van de Velde, the Elder

planking was observed, attached to squared oak frames. The southernmost section consisted of further planking attached to frames. Roundwood sticks and fine branches were found stuffed between the frames. This may have been dunnage (packing material used to prevent the movement of cargo or stores). A sample of an oak frame, including treenails, was recovered for dendrochronological dating and analysis. The dating was not conclusive but indicated that it was from a British tree felled sometime after 1639 (Nayling 2005a, 3).

Further diving in 2008 recorded a large section of coherent timber structure up to one metre high in the northern section of wreckage. An area of featureless seabed separated this from the central section of coherent timber structure which consisted of heavily eroded large planks and frames. Fragments of roundwood, probably dunnage, were also found.

Diving in 2005 on Site 5019 focused on two of three anomalies detected in sidescan sonar and multibeam surveys. The western anomaly was identified as a large pile of modern chain, with the link size of c 100mm suggesting a fairly small vessel. The chain ran off to the south and the PLA dive team concluded that it probably led to an anchor (PLA 2005d). More recent diving operations have identified a stud link chain leading off from the mound towards the east. Stud link chain suggests a date no earlier than the 19th century (Curryer 1999, 98–9).

The eastern anomaly consisted of distinct north and south sections (Fig. 19). Disturbed fragments of wood were found mixed with modern debris over a wide area, including a plain chamfered deck beam of 250–300mm sided and a possible truck wheel or pulley block.

The most remarkable discovery in 2005 was a 9 foot (2.74m) long bronze cannon, lying on roundwood. The bore of the gun was 4 inches wide (102mm) which led the archaeologist concerned to identify it as a saker or demi-culverin. No obvious decoration was felt on the surface of the gun. Figure 19 shows where this discovery is now thought to have been made (Wessex Archaeology 2012a, fig. 3). The gun was one of perhaps 40 unaccounted for at the time.

Further diving investigations were carried out at Site 5019 following reports of unauthorised salvage of cannon from the site in 2007 (Fig. 6). In the northern section of the eastern anomaly, a dense scatter of broken timber structure with some metal objects and handmade bricks was recorded, as well as organic matter including leather and possible sandbags. Sheets of lead, a well-preserved cleat and a brass or copper alloy ring were also reported, together with a musket butt. Substantial structural timbers from a wooden ship were found, including a 3m beam and a 5m long run of planking, particularly along the eastern edge, together with a large anchor ring with a diameter of 0.9m (Wessex Archaeology 2008b, 2–3). The cannon found in 2005 was not relocated.

The objects and ship structure recorded on the seabed suggested the presence of a partially broken up wreck with much debris and some sections of coherent structure. The musket butt has been identified as being from a matchlock musket dating to 1640–1670 and is typical of guns of the period immediately following the English Civil War (J. Ferguson, Royal Armouries, pers. comm.).

Two bronze cannon were reported by the 2007 salvors as having been recovered from the London. The first was an English demi-cannon cast by George Browne in 1656–7 as part of a set made for the London and possibly its sister ship the Dunbar. The second was a 24-pounder cast in c 1595 by Peter Gill as a culverin but later re-bored (Fox 2012, 73). Both guns are now in the collection of the Royal Armouries.

Three other bronze guns were reported by the salvors as having been recovered from another site in international waters. These are all 24-pounders cast for the defences of Amsterdam between 1600 and 1617 (Fox 2012, 73–4). Rather strangely, the bore of the cannon located in 2005 in 5019 is considerably smaller than that of any of the cannon salvaged in 2007. Whilst it is conceivable that this gun remains on site, it has not been located despite several searches and the most likely explanation is that the bore measurement was affected by the difficult diving conditions. The George Browne demi-cannon may well be that gun.

Subsequent diving and geophysical survey has been carried out on behalf of English Heritage in relation to the Protection of Wrecks Act (1973), and more recently by a local volunteer group.

It has become clear through these diving investigations that Site 5019 comprises two very different wrecks, with the southern section of the main eastern wreck area now positively identified as a later wreck. A large section of the hull of a small and probably flat-bottomed wooden vessel has been identified with typical 19th-century construction features. These include iron beam brackets and cuprous fastenings. Chemical analysis of one of the fastenings has indicted that it is Muntz metal and therefore unlikely to date from before the widespread adoption of that metal in the 1840s.

To the north of this, a far more substantial section of ship structure is present, with evidence of well-preserved outer and inner planking, frames and knees. This section of hull is particularly apparent on the east side where the edge of the structure is exposed but may also extend to the west side where less coherent planking and framing has been recorded (as with all London Gateway sites restricted visibility means that examination and identification is often a slow and only partial process). This section of hull may measure more than 12m across and appears to underpin a large area of debris. This includes roundwood which is thought likely to be firewood, a large quantity of rigging or anchor rope and a number of partially preserved barrels.

The probable cookroom bricks previously reported in 2007 lay within this area and current thinking suggests that this is part of the hold of the London and its well-preserved contents. If so, they may provide archaeological confirmation of what we hitherto can only infer from contemporary specifications of large Commonwealth warships, that until the mid-1660s the cookroom hearth of English ships of this period would have been placed on a platform on false beams in the forward hold just before the main hatch (Fox 2012, 61). It would also be consistent with the presence of rope, which would probably have been kept on cable tiers or elsewhere within the hold, and the presence of barrels.

Test pits excavated to obtain hull timber samples for dendrochronology in 2010, the results of which were not available at the time of writing, also resulted in the discovery of an intact glass 'shaft and globe' bottle from an undisturbed organic silt context within this section of the site (Fig. 21). The bottle dates to 1650–1680 (Wessex Archaeology 2011f, 17). Its rounded shoulder suggests that it dates to around 1660 (Biddle and Webster 2005, 267).

Perhaps the most remarkable discovery from 5019 is that of the remains of two to three people. Human remains are fairly rare discoveries on shipwreck sites and tend to occur as isolated finds of individual bones. The *London* sank with great loss of life and perhaps it is not so surprising that they have been found. What is remarkable, however, is the fact that probably two of the people found were women.

Women would not have formed part of the crew at this date but they were allowed on board in port and also whilst the ships were travelling to and from anchorages, in other words whilst the ship was mustering with a fleet (Davies 2008, 156). Pepys' diary entry mentioned that a woman was amongst the few survivors and the women found are therefore likely to have been the wives or partners of the crew (or possibly prostitutes) and would have been put ashore when Lawson's fleet sailed against the Dutch. It was therefore their misfortune that the accident occurred when it did.

Site 5029 is currently believed to contain the partially buried remains of one or more sections of the *London's* lower hull. Parametric sonar and probe surveys carried out in 2010 have demonstrated that the archaeological deposits associated with this site are likely to be one metre or more deep in places and extend beyond the boundaries of the archaeological material exposed on the seabed surface (Wessex Archaeology 2011f, 12 and 14).

A large green-glazed post-medieval Spanish olive jar sherd was found in 2010. Such jars, made in the Seville area, have a wide distribution across Europe. The earliest examples date to the 1580s and trade lasted well into the 18th century (Hurst *et al.* 1986, 66).

Warships of this period rarely carried the same armament through their entire careers and much is known from Ordnance Board records about the changing armament of the *London*. What has, however, come as a surprise is the discovery in 2011–12 of at least 11 heavily concreted iron guns in the central section of 5029. The discovery of these guns initially caused some surprise as the *London* is known from the Chatham ordnance journal to have been armed with an all bronze armament on 23 February 1665 (Fox 2012, 67).

Figure 21: Shaft and globe type bottle dating to 1650–1680 from Site 5019, the *London*

Large iron cannon were difficult to cast reliably at this time and had an alarming tendency to burst without warning, killing or seriously injuring anyone nearby. This obviously made them less than popular with gunners. Bronze guns tended to bulge and give fair warning that they were about to fail but were far more expensive to cast because of the cost of the metal.

Documentary evidence suggests that the late 17th-century salvor William Harrington recovered iron guns from the site (Fox 2012, 68). The *London* is known from other contemporary documents to have been reballasted before it sailed and the fact that this ballast came from upriver of Deptford rather than from Chatham also suggests that it was something unusual. Given that the iron guns on the *London* site are lying on what appears to be part of the hull of the ship and also appear to be loosely stacked, it is likely that the unusual ballast consisted of worn out or otherwise scrap Stuart or even Tudor guns, possibly despatched from the Ordnance Office stores at the Tower of London (Fox 2012, 68). If this is correct, then they are rare and potentially important examples of early English iron artillery. The Estuary has certainly produced other important evidence of early English artillery, such as the four iron guns recovered from the Gresham Ship, including a rare example of an early (16th century) English saker.

The presence of iron guns on a ship known to have carried an all bronze armament does raise the possibility that the wreck has been misidentified. However, the only losses of the correct date so far traced are the four fireships expended by the English during a battle against the blockading Dutch fleet near the Buoy of the Nore in 1667. Those vessels were destroyed by fire, for which there is currently no evidence at either 5019 or 5029. Although they carried an armament of iron guns, they would have been disposed for action and this is inconsistent with the current disposition of the guns found on 5029. Furthermore no iron guns have been found on 5019. Whilst the possibility that the wreck of one or more of these fireships has been mistaken for part of the London cannot be discounted, it appears very unlikely.

The presence of guns used as ballast also suggests that 5029 contains a large part of the hold. It may well be the case that the well preserved and relatively lightly built structure also found represents the collapsed remains of the internal timber structure of the ship. Furthermore the north-south orientation of the guns and the fact that the longest axis of 5029 is similarly orientated suggests that the fore and aft axis of the vessel lies on a north-south axis. There is also some indication from the geophysical and diving data that a single large section of hull may underpin much of 5029, in which case it may represent where Pepys describes the ship as having settled on the seabed after the explosion.

Investigations undertaken for London Gateway and subsequently have demonstrated that 5019 and particularly 5029 have a rich and diverse artefact assemblage. The excellent preservation of parts of wooden objects (Wessex Archaeology 2011; 2012a) and the presence of human remains suggests that this may be due to a good preservation environment just below the surface. Unfortunately, the fact that so much delicate and vulnerable material lies exposed on the seabed surface, and the changes in depth recorded during hydrographic surveys of the late 20th century and continuing bathymetric surveys carried out for London Gateway, indicate that the site is not stable. At the present time the environment is predominantly depositional, although some localised erosion is occurring. Direct observations by the local volunteer dive team that is currently studying the site (including a dive programme in 2012) suggest significant short-term changes of a type that is very difficult to monitor through even high resolution bathymetric surveys.

The work carried out on both Sites 5019 and 5029 for London Gateway have established the presence of what may be considered an important post-medieval wreck in the Thames Estuary.

The survey and investigation carried out have been instrumental in developing marine archaeological techniques applicable in inhospitable marine environments. Notably, the use of diver tracking and positional techniques were proved invaluable in establishing the nature and extent of wreck remains when working in zero visibility. It was ultimately these investigations which laid the foundations for the recognition of the importance of this wreck and its designation under the Protection of Wrecks Act (1973). In addition to building on the results achieved during London Gateway work, the subsequent work carried out for English Heritage has demonstrated the value of the type of longer diving investigations than are undertaken during schemes such as London Gateway. It has also demonstrated the value of other geophysical survey techniques that are rarely deployed in an archaeological context.

The wreck of the London has provided, and is continuing to reveal, key data on the nature of post-medieval naval warfare and maritime defence such as the layout of warships and the activities on board. In particular, as a discrete 17th-century social group, the human remains of the women, seamen and officers on board are likely to be of considerable research potential and may make a useful comparison with the group of sailors and marines recovered from the burial ground of the Royal Hospital Greenwich (Boston et al. 2008).

As well as ensuring that the scheme did not impact a nationally important wreck, work on the London carried out for London Gateway or that has flowed from it has answered some of the questions that surround this important wreck, and represents the first systematic archaeological investigation of a large English warship of the Commonwealth or early Restoration period.

Wooden sailing vessels in the 19th and early 20th centuries

The 19th and early 20th centuries are arguably the most important period in British commercial maritime history. It was a period of revolutionary change and extraordinary growth, when the full impact of the industrial revolution and of Britain's commercial and colonial expansion was felt.

The widespread adoption of steam power and the shift from wooden to iron and then steel hulls that occurred in the late 19th century resulted in the development of much larger and specialised sea-going cargo vessels. The expansion of commerce increased exponentially the number of vessels engaged in foreign-going trade and by the 1870s the merchant tonnage clearing British ports was greater than that of the other three major European maritime nations combined (Simper 1982, 61). This expansion was mirrored by that of coastal trade and the total tonnage carried coastwise regularly exceeded that shipped out of the country (Jackson 1983, 114). Rising demand for food in the growing industrial centres also stimulated a rapid growth in the fishing industry.

The estuary of the Thames was the gateway to the largest and most important port in the world, London. The tonnage of foreign-going vessels entering or clearing the port increased by a factor of 250% between 1873 and 1913 (Starkey 1999, 158–9). The city had always been the destination of most of the coastal trade in the UK and its growth and that of industrial and population centres in its hinterland resulted in the tonnage of coastal vessels entering or clearing the port of London increasing by almost 325% during the same period (ibid.). Coastal towns around the Thames Estuary underwent rapid development and local industries, such as the brickworks concentrated in the Sittingbourne area of Kent, flourished. Coastal trade from smaller towns contributed to an increase in maritime traffic throughout the Estuary (Brandon and Short 1990, 302).

Figure 22: Thames bawleys at Gravesend in 1881

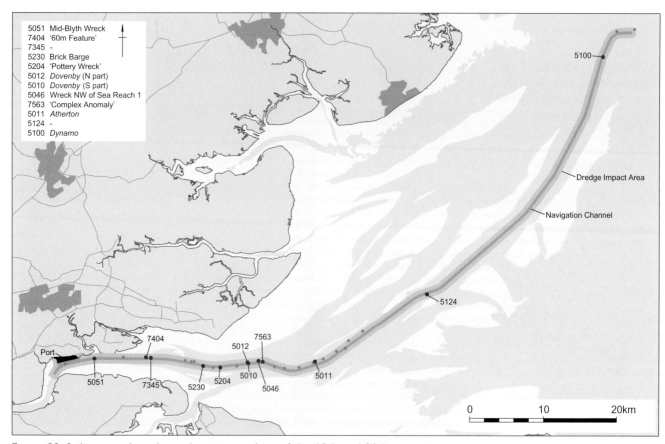

5051	Mid-Blyth Wreck
7404	'60m Feature'
7345	-
5230	Brick Barge
5204	'Pottery Wreck'
5012	*Dovenby* (N part)
5010	*Dovenby* (S part)
5046	Wreck NW of Sea Reach 1
7563	'Complex Anomaly'
5011	*Atherton*
5124	-
5100	*Dynamo*

Figure 23: Sailing vessels and merchant steam ships of the 19th and 20th centuries

The vessels using the Estuary will have been representative of many important developments in merchant ship design, technology and use. They will also be representative of the final perfection of sailing ship technology, as well as many different types of small vernacular coastal and fishing vessels. There are a number of important regional types, including the many different types of Thames barge used in coastal trade and the various wherries and bawleys used for fishing (Simper 1997, 60–100; Fig. 22).

The Estuary has many shifting sandbanks and its approaches are potentially hazardous. Large numbers of vessels are known to have been lost during the 19th century. For example, 74 strandings are known from Board of Trade records to have occurred on Gunfleet Sands between 1860 and 1869 alone and research for the Thames Estuary Dredging Association Regional Environmental Assessment has revealed that between 1816 and 1913 over 1000 losses occurred in the northern approaches to the Estuary off Essex and Suffolk (Wessex Archaeology 2010c, 53).

The scale of these losses is an indicator that the Estuary is potentially rich in the archaeology of 19th- and early 20th-century maritime commerce and fishing. Despite this very few actual 19th- and early 20th-century wrecks are known. For example, virtually none are recorded by the NRHE records for the period 1860–1913 (Wessex Archaeology 2011a, 28).

Research into wrecks of the late 19th and early 20th centuries has also demonstrated that very few wrecks of this period have been investigated archaeologically. For example, only 0.5% of the known wrecks recorded in England by the NRHE as having been lost between 1860 and 1913 have been archaeologically investigated (*ibid.*, 32).

It is not surprising, therefore, that until the London Gateway scheme little archaeological attention had been given to subtidal 19th- and early 20th-century cargo and fishing vessels in the Estuary. What had been done tended to be intertidal sites, for example in relation to the hulks at Whitewall Creek in the Medway (Milne *et al.* 1998) and the five 19th-century lighters investigated at Erith on the River Thames (Dawkes *et al.* 2009).

The London Gateway investigations have been directed by a fixed study area rather than by a research agenda. This has presented the archaeologists involved with an opportunity to refocus archaeological attention away from traditional pre-occupations with vessels of the pre-Modern, particularly warships, towards wrecks of the type and period that are in fact most commonly encountered at sea, that is, vessels of the 19th and 20th centuries. As a result, whilst only two to three post-medieval wreck sites were investigated by the scheme, many more 19th- or 20th-century wrecks have been located and investigated (Fig. 23).

The results of ten of these investigations are considered below. These include coastal trading vessels of distinctly regional character, a local type of fishing boat, a late 19th-century ocean-going sailing ship and examples of the type of steamship that supplanted it.

Wooden sailing vessels

During the mid-19th century, the use of metal freed shipbuilders from the design constraints of using timber, allowing larger, faster, more capacious and safer cargo vessels to be built. As a result the late 19th century saw a permanent transition from a merchant fleet built predominantly of wood to one built of iron and steel (Ville 1993, 52).

This did not, however, mean the end of the wooden ship. In the late 19th-century metal hulls were still used mainly for foreign-going vessels, in trades which took them to larger commercial ports (*ibid.*). Smaller ports were often not equipped to handle the maintenance and repair requirements of iron vessels. Wooden vessels could serve a wide variety of cargoes and destinations and in the coastal trade large numbers of barges and other wooden vessels continuing to travel between London, Essex, Kent and further afield. Records show that between 1860 and 1913 26% of all wrecks, for which information is available, are wooden vessels (Wessex Archaeology 2011a, 37). For the period between 1914 and 1938 this figure is reduced to just 5% (Wessex Archaeology 2011b, 7).

Despite the presence of a large number of identified wooden wrecks in UK waters (146 dated to 1860–1913 in territorial waters off England alone; Wessex Archaeology 2011a, 10) there are few examples of wrecks that have been studied archaeologically and published. Examples, such as the 19th-century wreck in Cardigan Bay misidentified as the merchant ship *Diamond* (Wessex Archaeology 2006d), the English East Indiamen *Earl of Abergavenny* off Dorset, the Whitewall Creek hulks and more recent examples such as the 1895 wreck of the Canadian barque Antoinette in the Camel Estuary (Johns *et al.* 2011) and the remarkably preserved wooden collier discovered on the Goodwin Sands (Wessex Archaeology 2012b), remain unusual. Outside the UK, the 19th-century wooden sailing ship engaged in bringing British coal to Rotterdam and recorded following clearance from the Slufter is a notable example from a development-led context similar to that of London Gateway (Adams *et al.* 1990, 71–134).

With so few investigated examples it is notable that seven of the sites investigated for London Gateway have been identified as the remains of wooden vessels.

Site 5046

(*c* 700m NW of Sea Reach 1 in the Estuary, *c* 6km off Shoeburyness; depth 13.3m, Figs 23–24)

Site 5046 was found on the north edge of the channel during a PLA hydrographic survey in 1990. Three small obstructions and an associated scour pit were detected (PLA 2005e). Sidescan sonar and magnetometer surveys in 2001 and 2002 were interpreted as showing a wreck-shaped object and the site was subsequently investigated by a PLA dive team in 2005 and a

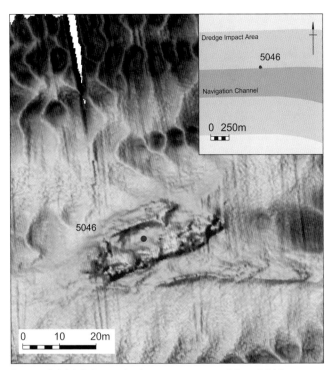

Figure 24: Multibeam bathymetry image of Site 5046, Unknown Wreck

multibeam survey later that year. A short archaeological diving investigation was carried out by Wessex Archaeology in 2007 as part of the scheme mitigation with further archaeological inspection dives carried out in 2008.

As the wreck was considered most likely to be late 19th or 20th century, it was cleared by grab dredger with an archaeological watching brief (Wragg 2010a–b).

In 2005, PLA divers reported many wood, metal and concrete objects (PLA 2005e) and later that year the multibeam survey showed a wreck-like anomaly up to 43m long and 16m wide (Fig. 24). In 2007 the site was confirmed as a wreck when Wessex Archaeology discovered worked timbers with metal fastenings together with fragments of what appeared to be riveted metal plate and chain. The wreck was more fully investigated in 2008.

Discovery of a 13m length of the hull proved what was apparent from the bathymetry data (Fig. 24), that the wreck was at least partly coherent and that it was a wooden framed and planked vessel. A ferrous knee or rider demonstrated that the vessel was built with a metal reinforced hull and that it was unlikely to have been built before the 19th century.

When the wreck was cleared, ship timbers with cuprous fastenings were recovered, including floor and framing timbers, part of an elaborate 'balustrade' (the upright part of the rail found on a raised forecastle or poop/quarter deck), hull planking, a rudder and a cast iron muzzle-loading cannon (Fig. 25).

The cuprous fastenings were initially dated to the late 19th century or later, although a more cautious view may be that they are unlikely to pre-date the 19th century. They were introduced in the late 18th century and were widely adopted by wooden shipbuilders in the

Figure 25: Cast iron cannon and Buchanan whisky bottle from Site 5046

19th century in place of the iron bolts previously used for framing. This was a response to the galvanic corrosion experienced with iron bolts used below the waterline following the introduction of copper sheathing.

While the ratio of rudder size to vessel size can be very variable (Campbell 1974, 153), Meade's 1869 *Treatise on Naval Architecture and Shipbuilding* states that:

> 'The way to give power to the rudder is to proportion it to the length of the ship, for a long ship requires a broad rudder. It is thought that for every 100 feet [30.48m] in the length of a ship she should have 2 feet [0.61m] of breadth with one foot [0.305m] added. Thus a ship of 100 feet long needs 3 feet breadth of rudder' (Meade 1869, 97).

Using Meade's guidance, the rudder recovered from this site suggests that the vessel would have had a length of 111 feet (33.83m). However a rudder of this size would have had 3–4 copper pintles. The rudder from Site 5046 has five, suggesting a vessel length of 150 feet (45.72m) long. Whilst there were no hard and fast rules with regard to such proportions and any resulting calculation of length is undoubtedly speculative, the figure derived does correspond remarkably closely to the overall length of the anomaly.

As no evidence has been found for an engine, it is reasonable to conclude that 5046 is the wreck of a vessel of a medium sized wooden sailing ship built in the 19th or very early 20th century. Its use is uncertain as no cargo or fittings indicative of a particular trade have been observed or recovered from the site although its use as a merchant ship is considered most likely. If so, it is of a size that would have enabled it to work in either the coastal or foreign-going trades. The absence of cargo is probably due to the vessel being in ballast at the time of loss or to subsequent salvage. Unless blown into the Estuary by an easterly storm, it is likely to have been sailing to or from London or one of the Estuary ports.

The cannon is a short 3-pounder of the Blomefield pattern, with a date range 1787–1822 (Wragg 2010b, 6). This gun is something of a puzzle. It is conceivable that the vessel could have been armed but if it is late 19th century or later then this is unlikely. It may have been onboard as a signal gun. It is also conceivable that it was being carried as ballast, in the same way that the much earlier *London* had carried such guns. Alternatively its presence may simply be co-incidental.

Date of loss is uncertain as the site has not so far been linked to any known casualty. Two glass bottles were recovered from the site during the 2008 diving operations. One was of green glass, moulded with the lettering 'Buchanans Black and White Whisky'. This drink was produced by James Buchanan from 1884 and the brand still exists (Fig. 25). The second bottle was a small brown glass short-necked beer bottle, shoulder-stamped 'No Deposit No Return' and base-stamped '0.33L PLM L18' and dates from the latter half of the 20th century. It seems unlikely that a late 20th century loss at this location would have gone unnoticed. Given that it is quite common in the Thames for intrusive modern material to be found on older wreck sites as a result of the action of tidal currents, there is a good chance that the presence of this bottle is coincidental.

The wreck located during investigation of Site 5046 for London Gateway may remain unidentified but the clearance of the remains under archaeological supervision has provided an assemblage of structural remains and artefacts that have been made available for further archaeological assessment. This assemblage offers a valuable opportunity to gain additional understanding of 19th-century wooden ships and shipping.

Site 5051

(*c* 300m S of Thames Haven anchorage, *c* 1km off Hole Haven; depth 13m, Figs 23, 26)

This site first came to light in 1996 when a vessel fouled its trawl gear. When recovered the gear had traces of rust from contact with the debris. A PLA team dived the site and reported 'old timber', reinforced concrete and other debris. It had been thought that it might be modern fly-dumping, but none of it appeared to be recently deposited.

The site was subject to sidescan survey for the scheme in 2001 and 2002 and multibeam survey in 2005 (Fig. 26). Further diving investigations were carried out by the PLA in 2005 and by Wessex Archaeology in 2007 and 2008. In 2008 the use of a large airlift that emptied onto the deck of the support vessel succeeded in recovering over 180 artefacts (Wessex Archaeology 2008c, 6).

Given the probable modern date of this wreck, it was not considered to be of sufficient importance to warrant *in situ* preservation or impact avoidance, and it was cleared by grab dredger in February 2010 under archaeological watching brief (Wragg 2010c).

Archaeological interpretation of the PLA multibeam data revealed a large mound with a very distinct rectangular-shaped object approximately 18m long by 4.5m wide (Wessex Archaeology 2008c, fig. 2). This object had one rounded-end and one irregular-end and was quite clearly a single partially intact wreck. Intrusive archaeological diving in 2007 identified the wreck as a wooden framed and planked vessel, although covered by loose sand and gravel.

A pottery flagon recovered from the seabed surface within the site bore the manufacturer's stamp: 'Doulton & Watts Lambeth Pottery'. Similar flagons appear in the manufacturer's price list of 1873 (DD/655/21) and this particular stamp was in use from the 1820s until 1854. A second stamp indicates the owner was 'F White Crown & Anchor Hotel Woolwich'. F. White is listed in a publican directory for the hotel in 1855. A refined whiteware Ironstone Montilla plate, stamped with poorly defined numerals of 1862 or 1882, a brown-glazed stoneware porter bottle with an intact cork stamped 'R & I White Sittingbourne' and a stoneware jar thought to be a bung jar, are also later 19th century in date and were found in what is thought to have been an *in situ* context within the hull (Fig. 27).

Evidence for ship's fittings included a possible brass latch and cuprous rings, probably part of a sheave or deadeye, and an intact wooden sheave rigging block. Barrel staves recovered may be evidence of cargo or may have been used to store the crew's food or rations. Possible personal possessions of the vessel's crew include several spade or shovel handles, one of the shovels roughly inscribed with the letters 'W' and 'D'. Several pieces of a leather boot and a leather shoe upper were also recovered (Fig. 27). A small quantity of coal was recovered, possibly intended for use in a stove, together

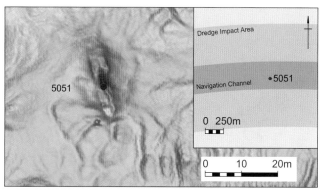

Figure 26: Multibeam bathymetry image of Site 5051, Unknown Wreck

with animal bone from cattle and sheep or goats. A large quantity of flint recovered may have been ballast as the surrounding seabed is sandy silt over clay.

A large number of fragmentary planks were recovered, along with floor timbers exhibiting evidence of mortise and tenon joints, framing timbers, timber knees, and sections of articulated planking, part of a bilge pump, much rope, flint gravels and pottery, including a sherd of 18th–19th-century creamware and a stoneware bottle manufactured by J. Price between 1850 and 1940.

The character of the timbers recovered during clearance suggests that 5051 was a stemheaded sailing barge, similar in character and size to the barges *Rathmona* and *Berwick* recorded at Whitewall Creek (Milne *et al.* 1998, 28 and 30–1). As a regional type, 5051 is likely to have been built within the Estuary and a transom stern timber recovered from Site 5051 is of a type used on Thames barges from about 1860 and suggests that the building of 5051 does not predate 1860 (Milne *et al.* 1998, 32). The date of loss is uncertain. The site has not been linked to any known loss. The recovered material suggests a date after *c* 1860 and possibly after 1882. The dates of the pottery, in particular the flagon suggest that a 20th century date is probably too late, although the possibility cannot be discounted. At the present time a post-1860 late 19th century date is likely.

Barges such as Site 5051 would have been used for coastal trade within the Estuary and further afield. No obvious cargo has been recovered and it has been speculated that some of the timbers recovered were being carried from a shipbreaking yard as cargo. The alternative explanation is that it was in ballast when lost, possibly having delivered a cargo to the Woolwich area.

It has been suggested that the site did not consist of a single intact vessel and that fragments of at least two and possibly three are present. The floor timbers have been attributed to a barge, the knees to another square-sectioned vessel and the sinuous frames to a fishing boat or bally (Wragg 2010c, 23). In addition it has been suggested that the apparent absence of evidence for a keel suggests that the remains are fragmentary. However, this is unlikely, as it is readily apparent from the geophysical data that the site consisted of the hull of a single vessel. That data demonstrates that one end of the

Figure 27: Objects recovered from Site 5051 including barrel parts, footwear, implement handles, and a sheave block

site is curved and appears to be intact and that the other, northern end is not intact, indicating that the barge was in fact longer than 18m. The most likely explanation for the presence of timbers that are not consistent with the design of the *Rathmona* and *Berwick* is perhaps that the design of 19th-century barges of this type was not as standardised as analysis of these fragmentary vessels suggests. The absence of a keel may simply be because it was not cleared.

Site 5051 is one of two sailing barges to have been examined for London Gateway (see also 5230). Although regional barge survivals are known from intertidal contexts and have been studied, the investigations carried out for London Gateway are thought to represent the first, although partial, archaeological examination of the largely intact wrecks of such a vessel at sea complete with its extensive and varied inventory and have contributed to our knowledge of coastal trade in the Thames Estuary. They also represent a contribution to a number of objectives in the *Greater Thames Estuary Historic Environment Research Framework* (2010), including (2A.AR10), the synthesising of data relating to Thames barges, and the role of seaborne trade (2a.SO2).

Site 5204 ('Pottery Wreck')

(*c* 1km E of Sea Reach 3, 4km due S of Shoeburyness; depth 14.5m, Figs 23, 28)

This site was first located during a PLA channel extension survey in 1999. It was not detected in sidescan surveys carried out for London Gateway in 2001 and 2002 but was detected as a low complex mound as a result of a multibeam survey in 2005 (Fig. 28; Wessex Archaeology 2008d, 7). The site was dived by the PLA in 2005 and twice by Nigel Nayling. Timber and pottery samples were recovered for identification and analysis. The site was subject to further diving investigation by the PLA and Wessex Archaeology in 2006 and a sidescan sonar survey was carried out in 2007. Intrusive diving work was undertaken by Wessex Archaeology in 2008 prior to clearance.

Initial diving investigation by the PLA suggested that it was the partially buried wreck of 'an old wooden boat', possibly clinker built, within a debris field (PLA 2005f). The subsequent archaeological diving inspection for London Gateway confirmed the presence of a wooden wreck and located a keel timber which was 7m in length. Small timber frames recovered by the PLA in 2005 were identified as oak (Nayling 2005b, 3). Two sherds of pottery were identified as post-medieval coarse redware fabrics, one a white slipped flared bowl and the other a handle stump from a large cup or porringer. Both are 19th- or early 20th-century in date (Wessex Archaeology 2008d, 7). The recovery of these led to the site being rather misleadingly known as the 'Pottery Wreck'.

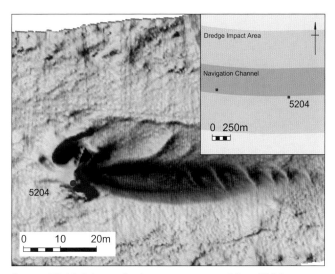

Figure 28: Multibeam bathymetry image of Site 5204, 'Pottery Wreck'

A dive by Wessex Archaeology in 2006 showed the keel to be rabetted, with evidence of several fresh breaks in the timber; intrusive diving work in 2008 revealed partially intact framing with inner and outer flush-laid planking covered by soft metal sheeting. Part of the sternpost was excavated and recovered to the surface. Overall, the recovered timbers comprised two sternpost timbers, part of the keel (double-rabetted with indications of both wooden and metal fastenings), five frames and five planks (Fig. 29). Part of the sternpost was in good condition and featured a tenon, which presumably joined it to the keelson, and ferrous concretion indicating a large iron fastening, probably a gudgeon. The five frames are undoubtedly clinker frames, with notches (joggles) where the planks fitted, representing both first and upper futtocks.

Nearly 300 finds were recovered to the surface (Wessex Archaeology 2008d, 10–12). These included stone, glass, ceramics, brick, metal, wood and bone. The glass included a 19th-century dark green glass bottle neck and a piece from the neck of a clear thin-walled vessel, possibly an oil lamp. Sherds of a brown glass 0.33 litre bottle with 'No Return' embossed on it are probably 20th century in date. Sherds of post-medieval coarse redware pottery were recovered, including a white-slipped and glazed flared bowl characteristic of Yorkshire and Newcastle wares of late 19th- to early 20th-century date, as well as pearlware, including a jug handle, and glazed red, yellow and refined whiteware. Recovered fragments of frogged bricks post-dated the early 19th century. Possible personal items included a bone knife handle incised with criss-cross decoration, the sole of a leather shoe, and a sailor's palm thimble.

The form of the frames suggests a 'wineglass'-shaped section with a minimum possible beam of 3.75m, suggestive of a bawley, a local fishing vessel of the 19th–20th centuries. Bawleys were a form of fishing smack. Gravesend bawleys (Fig. 22) were generally clinker-built, primarily used for shrimping, and were equipped with a copper for boiling the shrimps (Simper 1997, 85). Bawleys of Southend and the Medway were

larger and carvel-constructed to allow them to fish further out in the estuary (*ibid.*, 86–8). Medway bawleys often had a removable mast to allow them to pass under Rochester Bridge, and were also used in dredging for Medway oysters.

The pottery recovered suggests that this bawley was probably lost in the first half of the 20th century. However, it has not been linked to any known loss. The investigation of a probable bawley is thought to represent the first archaeological recording of the wreck of this type of regional vernacular boat, once common in the Estuary. Fishing vessels, particularly those of small size, are very poorly represented in the national stock of wrecks (Wessex Archaeology 2011a, 60). Bawleys are not recorded, although there are a number in preservation, including a Gravesend bawley (National Small Boats Register). Site 5204 was therefore an important discovery and demonstrates the need for the investigation of fishing vessels to be integrated within the existing regional research framework.

Site 5230 (Brick Barge)

(*c* 1.3km W of Sea Reach 3, *c* 4km SW of Shoeburyness; depth 12.3m, Figs 23, 30)

This site was charted on the south side of the channel between Sea Reach 3 and 4 by the UKHO as the possible remains of a brick barge. This was based on letters received by the PLA regarding the sinking of such a vessel in 1922. Three anomalies were identified in the sidescan sonar surveys for London Gateway in 2001 and 2002 (7540, 7128 and 7224). Diving by the PLA in 2005 reconciled the position of 7224 with the location of the brick barge, Site 5230 and the site was dived by Nigel Nayling later that year. The PLA carried out a multibeam survey of the site in 2006 and further diving investigations were carried out by Wessex Archaeology in 2008. The site was cleared under archaeological supervision by grab dredger in February 2010.

Multibeam survey of Site 5230 in 2005 identified a 12m by 4m mound with a smaller area of debris to the south (Fig. 30). Diving investigations located piles of bricks, some of which were neatly stacked, together with timber and metal features that were considered to be consistent with the presence of a wreck (Nayling 2005b, 2–3). A number of London stock bricks that were recovered had a rudimentary frog and were stamped with 'DKB'. They are likely to have been manufactured

Figure 29: Selection of timbers recovered from Site 5204 ('Pottery Wreck'), including frames and part of the keel

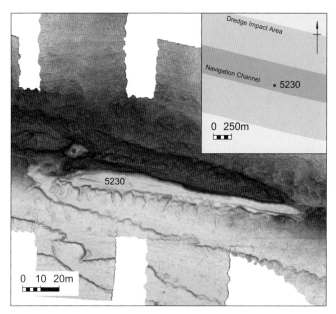

Figure 30: Multibeam bathymetry image of Site 5230, Brick Barge

in Kent, post-1850 (Wessex Archaeology 2007a, 2). Two metal bars, one L-shaped, were recovered (PLA 2005g). These may be metal reinforcements for the wooden hull of a vessel.

During clearance, structural elements, comprising mortised floor timbers, partially articulated framing, planks and fragments were recovered, possibly part of the vessel's deadwood and rudder. Bricks, rope, concreted chain, two ferrous rowlocks, an anchor and a possible bilge pump were also recovered (Wragg 2010d). The anchor was a rounded crown 'Admiralty' pattern anchor with what appeared to be an iron stock and is consistent with the second half of the 19th- or 20th-century date.

The various timbers recovered were consistent with the structure of the stern of a Thames sailing barge. The floor timbers are reported to have been similar to those recorded in the 1906 built stemheaded barge *Berwick* in Whitewall Creek and deadwood similar to the 1863 sailing barge *Aline*, also in Whitewall (*ibid.*, 29; Milne *et al.* 1998, 32 and 45–7). It is likely that 5230 is the unidentified barge lost in the Thames in 1922 whilst carrying a cargo of bricks.

It has been suggested that the failure to recover the keel reported by divers indicates that the wreck had previously been dredged and that it was therefore no longer coherent (Wragg 2010d, 29). This is possible but it is perhaps also plausible that the keel along with other parts of the vessel were not cleared from the site.

As noted for Site 5051, the study of sailing barges has contributed to our archaeological understanding of regional coastal shipping and represents the first such investigations of barges lost in use, with its inventory, rather than as an empty and abandoned hulk in an intertidal context.

Steel hulls and steam power

One of the key maritime technological developments of the 19th century was the development of steam power as an alternative means to sail. By freeing ships from dependence upon the wind, steamships offered lower operating costs and faster, safer passages (Thomas 1992, 11). The higher costs of building and operating steamships were offset by the need to hold lower stocks of goods as the quicker passages enabled more regular vessel movements. Improvements in engine technology such as the more efficient triple expansion steam engine, the more widespread introduction of bunkering and, crucially, the adoption of the screw propeller resulted in a tipping point being reached in the 1870s when sail was finally supplanted as the dominant force.

As discussed above, the 19th century also saw the transition from wood to iron and then to steel in shipbuilding. By the beginning of the 20th century, very few commercial ships were being built of wood and its use almost entirely died out after World War I (Wessex Archaeology 2011c, 7). The transition from sail to steam and from wood to iron, however, did not necessarily take place at the same time. Late 19th- and early 20th-century commercial sailing ships were often built with iron or steel hulls while early steam ships might still be built of wood. Wooden hulls and sail power also persisted in the smaller vessels built for coastal trade.

Major changes to the organisation of maritime trade took place during the 19th century including the introduction of submarine telegraph cables that for the first time allowed return cargoes to be organised in advance. The ability of the new steamships to sail to regular schedules resulted in the division of merchant shipping into the scheduled 'liner' and the opportunistic 'tramping' trades. From this developed the classic 'cargo liner', a vessel often optimised for speed and designed to carry a mix of general cargo and passengers; and the classic 'tramp ship', designed to carry bulk or general goods and operated to no fixed schedule, instead carrying cargoes of opportunity. Vessels could alternate between the liner and tramp trades, although distinct designs did gradually emerge.

The tramp dominated commercial shipping worldwide between the late 19th and mid-20th centuries and a good case can be made for it being the most important commercial vessel type ever developed. Despite this, almost no archaeological work has been done in connection with tramp ships, an absence that is reflected in the fact that the NRHE does not record either tramps or cargo liners as separate vessel types (*ibid.*, 40–1). This reflects a wider lack of archaeological research into steamship wrecks in the UK prior to London Gateway, in contrast to archaeologists in the United States and Australia who have made considerable efforts to engage with the archaeology of the steamship (McCarthy 2010, by way of example).

The Thames Estuary is a potentially rich source of evidence for this technological and commercial revolution that occurred at sea in the 19th century.

Sites 5010 and 5012 (Dovenby)

(c 1km E of Sea Reach 2, 5.5km off Shoeburyness, Figs 23, 31)

The wreck of the *Dovenby* is charted in two sections on the seabed, Site 5010 and, 160m away to the NNW, 5012 (Fig. 31, Wessex Archaeology 2007c). In 1967, a 5.8m upright section of mast was recovered from Site 5010 as it was posing a hazard to navigation. Later that year the site was cleared to a depth of 12.2m, and subsequently drift swept on several occasions.

Both sites were subject to sidescan survey for London Gateway in 2001 and 2002 and multibeam survey in 2005 (Fig. 31). Eight further anomalies were also identified during the course of geophysical survey. Anomalies 7368 and 7369 were located directly between 5010 and 5012. Four of the anomalies (7371, 7370, 7708 and 7140) were located approximately 140m to the west of 5010 and 5012. Anomaly 7139 is located approximately 230m to the west of 5010 and was only located during the 2001 sidescan survey. The latter was believed to be modern material that had since been removed or buried.

Both 5010 and 5012 were dived by the PLA and by Nigel Nayling in 2005. In 2006 the sites were dived by the PLA and Wessex Archaeology with a further diving investigation on Site 5012 in 2007.

The *Dovenby* lies in the centre of the navigation channel and covers a large area of seabed (200m by 200m, if all the anomalies associated with the sites are included). The investigations raised no doubts as to the identification of Site 5010 as being the *Dovenby*, although the identity of 5012 remained less certain. The diving that did take place on Site 5012 showed that considerably more time would be required to confirm the identity of the vessel; due to the difficulites of diving the sites, lack of visibility, its size, its lack of diagnostic features and the broken up character of the wreckage, further archaeological recording was considered to be unwarranted.

As such, and with the advice of English Heritage, no further work was planned for 5010/5012. However, clearance of the site was undertaken with archaeological supervision from Wessex Archaeology in connection with filming by Touch Productions on the two-part series *Thames Shipwrecks: a race against time*, which was aired on BBC2 (26 August/2 September 2008).

The three-masted steel-hulled barque *Dovenby* is representative of the late 19th century perfection of commercial sailing ship design (Fig. 32). It was built for P. Iredale and Porter Ltd by W. Pickersgill and Sons in the major shipbuilding centre of Sunderland in 1891 (Lloyds Register). The ship had a length of 78m and a beam of 11.6m. Gross registered tonnage was 1654. The *Dovenby's* first major voyage in 1891–2 took it from Middlesborough to Sydney and thence on to San Francisco. As a sailing ship it is likely to have been engaged in the tramping trade. The use of a steel hull provided the ship with all the advantages of metal

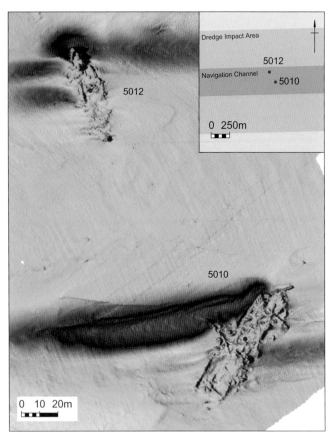

Figure 31: Multibeam bathymetry image of Sites 5010 and 5012, *Dovenby* North and South

construction, including cargo capacity and strength, but the choice of sail suggests that the bulk trades for which it seems to have been intended did not require the advantages of steam propulsion.

On 6 November 1914, *Dovenby* was *en route* from Peru to London laden with guano when it sank after colliding with the steamship *Sindoro* in a thick fog. Most of the vessel, except the vertical frames and ribs is reported to have been dispersed by explosives in 1915 (PLA 2005h). Following an inspection the wreck was blown up and portions removed or further dispersed in 1924 and 1967.

The 2005 multibeam survey showed that Site 5010 was clearly ship-shaped, measuring about 80m long by 13–15m wide (Fig. 31) with a deep scour pit on its western side. Site 5012 was observed to be about 55m long with a width of 12–15m. It had a very deep scour pit at its northern end. Numerous small anomalies in the vicinity were interpreted as possible debris.

The PLA dives in 2005 revealed steel structure, including exposed steel frames, large sections of which had been cut away, and possibly part of a rudder. The PLA report states that 5012 was the stern section and 5010 the bow, presumably because the rudder was found in the former. Site 5010 was reported to be in a deep scour, which is consistent with the multibeam, and on its side. The remains at Site 5012 was reported to be upright, which again appears consistent with the multibeam data.

Further dives on Site 5010 recorded riveted steel plates, presumably part of the outer hull of the vessel,

Figure 32: The three-masted barque *Dovenby*

standing *c* 1m proud of the seabed, a ship's bollard and a long cylindrical steel object, probably part of a steel mast. Site 5012 also included various distorted sections of riveted steel plates upstanding by 2–3m. A largely clear area towards the southern edge of the site was thought likely to be the gap in wreck structure noted in the multibeam data. No archaeological features were observed which would indicate the presence of a bow or stern (Wessex Archaeology 2007b).

Although the archaeological remains noted at Sites 5010 and 5012 are broadly similar they are a substantial distance apart and, given the size of each section, it is difficult to reconcile their positions with explosive dispersal or post-wrecking site formation processes. Furthermore, the geophysical data suggests that Site 5010 is 80m long, which approximates the length of the ship. Site 5012 is 55m long, making a total of 135m. Even taking into account dispersal and elongation as the wreck has collapsed, it is difficult to reconcile both as being the *Dovenby*. As the southern Site 5010 corresponds to the dimensions of the *Dovenby* it is possible that the northern site is the wreckage of another unknown vessel.

Although no further work was carried out prior to clearance, the *Dovenby* represented a rare opportunity to record the still substantial remains of a late 19th-century merchant ship *in situ*. During the course of the investigations data was accumulated which now forms the record of that site and part of the record of 19th-century shipping in the Thames Estuary, including media footage of the clearance which itself contributes to raising awareness of maritime archaeology in the Thames.

It is unfortunate that the difficult nature of diving at the site did not allow for further investigation to take place as part of the London Gateway scheme. Nevertheless, it does provide an example of how, despite difficulties, London Gateway allowed for the opportunistic recording of wreck sites as defined as a specific research objective in the *Greater Thames Estuary Historic Environment Research Framework* 2010 (Framework Object 2A.AR9).

Site 5011 (*Atherton*)

(Seaward of Sea Reach 1; Oaze Deep, *c* 12km off Foulness; depth 17.8m, Figs 23, 33)

The site was located outside the 2001 and 2002 survey areas but was seen in the 2005 multibeam survey undertaken by the PLA. Sidescan sonar survey of the site was undertaken in 2007. No diving investigations were carried out. No further archaeological investigation has taken place as the site lies outside the navigation channel and will be avoided by clearance activities. It was buoyed and left *in situ*.

Atherton was a screw-propelled, steel-hulled steamship equipped with a triple expansion three-cylinder engine, built in Vlaardingen in the Netherlands in 1918 and originally named *Arnhem*. After being acquired by the Gower Shipping Company of Swansea, *Atherton* worked as a general cargo vessel in the coastal and home trades. The surviving vessel structure, shown by the geophysical surveys, suggests that it was a typical coastal and home trade commercial steamship of the type that could have been engaged in both tramping and the liner trade.

Having narrowly escaped disaster when it collided with the steamer *Grampian* in the Thames on 20 January 1921 (Lloyds List, 21 January 1921), *Atherton* was lost

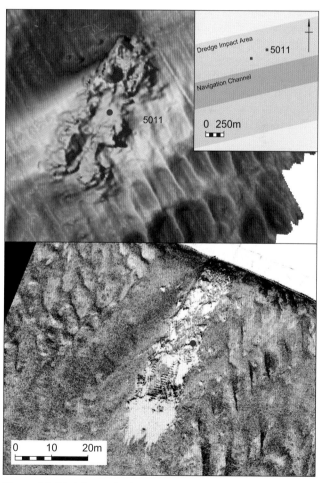

Figure 33: Multibeam bathymetry and sidescan images of Site 5011, *Atherton*

later that year on Christmas Day. It developed a heavy list after its deck cargo shifted and then sank near the Middle Ouse buoy after being abandoned (Lloyd's Weekly Casualty Reports, 2 January 1922).

The wreck was reported to have been partly dispersed using explosives by a Royal Navy team in 1959 (PLA 2005i). The multibeam survey showed a rectangular anomaly 45m long by 20m wide and up to 3m high (Fig. 33). The vessel appears to be partially intact and does not appear dispersed. The bathymetric high point is towards the northern end, possibly representing the funnel.

The sidescan sonar survey confirmed the information gathered from the multibeam data and shows the wreck broken up but intact at the western end with some structure showing. Debris associated with the wreck is seen as a number of small features up to 1m diameter.

No photographs of the vessel have been traced but a plan of the hull suggests that the design of the vessel incorporated a forward hold and an amidships bridge and engine and therefore funnel, although it could have been displaced during clearance or sweeping.

As no diving investigations have been carried out at Site 5011, its potential to provide archaeological insights into the coastal and home trade vessels of the early 20th century, and the mature steam technology represented by them, remains unclear and a subject for future investigation. Nevertheless, further archaeological investigation of the *Atherton* could offer an opportunity to undertake future research on the nature of cargoes and their movements in relations to local and more distant trade in line with the *Greater Thames Estuary Historic Environment Research Framework* 2010. The wreck may also contain evidence of life on board the vessel at the time of loss.

Site 5100 (*Dynamo*)

(*c* 21km off the Naze, near Harwich, Figs 23, 34)

The site was located outside the 2001 and 2002 survey areas but was subject to multibeam survey in 2006 undertaken by the PLA. Sidescan sonar survey of the site was undertaken in 2007. No diving investigations were carried out. No further archaeological investigation has taken place. The site lies 50m inside the navigation channel.

The 809 gross ton, 56m long *Dynamo* (Figs 34 and 35) was a screw-driven steam coaster, built by R. Williamson and Son of Workington in 1920, a company that mainly built for their own fleet. Fitted with a three-cylinder triple expansion engine, probably fuelled by coal, it incorporated many of the builder's own distinctive design features, such as the use of cargo hatches with curved sides that allowed for the trimming of bulk cargoes (Waine and Fenton 1994).

However, this vessel was built for Ellerman's Wilson Line, a Hull shipping company founded as The Wilson Line by Thomas Wilson in 1843 (Harrower 1998; Talbot-

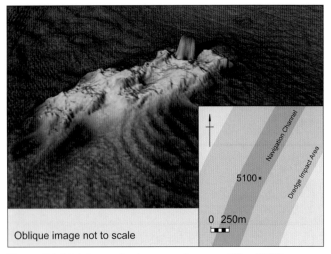

Figure 34: Multibeam bathymetry image of Site 5100, *Dynamo*

Booth 1940), which operating out of a number of ports, including London. *Dynamo* may have been engaged in the bulk coal trade as it is recorded as having sailed to the Newcastle area from London before then sailing to Rouen in May 1920 (Lloyd's List). If so then it is quite likely that it was operated, at least initially as a tramp.

The subsequent inter-war career of *Dynamo* has not been traced. However, during World War II it was one of 5500 merchant ships to have been defensively equipped and manned by personnel from the Royal Navy and Royal Artillery Maritime Regiment (Morison 1975, 301).

It was carrying military personnel when sunk by a mine on 17 April 1943 in the Thames Estuary (Lloyds of London), about 1.5km off the B8 Buoy in the Barrow Deep. It was reportedly carrying 15 crew and five passengers, listed as DEMS (Defensively Equipped Merchant Ship) Gunners. Four crew and three passengers were lost.

In 1959 the wreck, which lay inside the channel, was surveyed and reported to be upright. In 1988 and again in 2000 it was reported to be largely buried. Several surveys reported that it was breaking or broken up and surrounded by a debris field, including a multibeam echosounder survey in 2005 (UKHO 14530). However, archaeological interpretation of the multibeam survey data acquired in 2006 suggests that whilst there were signs that it was breaking up, the hull was still at least partially intact. The anomaly was 56m long, which corresponds exactly with the length of the *Dynamo*, and there appears to be only limited lateral spreading in parts (Fig. 34). Part of the height of the funnel of this

Figure 35: Photograph of the *Dynamo* at sea

aft-engine vessel was *in situ* or within a short distance of its expected position and standing to a height of over 4m. There were also clear signs that the bridge superstructure, which would have been just forward of amidships, was still partly in place. The location of the main impact of the mine is not readily apparent.

The site represents a fairly late manifestation of a long-lived 19th-century design of commercial steamship and a typical small early inter-war merchant ship. Although it was built at a time when commercial ship design was very slowly turning to motor ships and steam turbines, coal was abundant and British ship owners favoured what they knew to be reliable. It is also representative of a shipbuilding bubble in the early inter-war years. This bubble, which led to a deep depression in the shipbuilding industry that lasted into the 1930s, resulted from over-optimism about the number of new vessels that would be required to make up war losses and support the recovery of world trade.

The wreck is also interesting in a sense because it is typical rather than unusual. Whilst it is clear from NRHE records that inter-war steamship wrecks are abundant in territorial waters off England (Wessex Archaeology 2011c, 14), they are not well studied archaeologically (*ibid.*, 27–28). Assuming that the ship worked at least partly as a tramp in the coal trade it is also representative of the late phase of a huge 19th- and 20th-century trade that has only recently started to be examined archaeologically in the UK (Wessex Archaeology 2009b).

Unknown remains (Sites 5124, 7345, 7404 and 7563)

Four possible sites (7345, 7404, 7563 and 5124) identified by geophysical survey and also dived are of uncertain character. Site 7345 (Fig. 36) provided only limited evidence for a vessel of post-medieval or later date, although its size could not be determined. Site 7404 could not be verified as a wreck and could equally be a feature of natural origin. Site 7563 is most probably a natural seabed feature and Site 5124 was not certainly identified as a wreck (possibly dumped material).

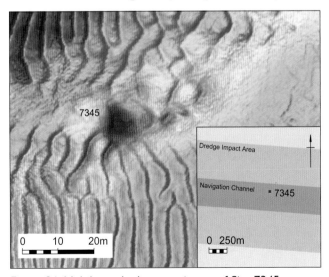

Figure 36: Multibeam bathymetry image of Site 7345

Twentieth century World Wars

The defence of the Thames Estuary during the two world wars of the 20th century was perhaps the most significant theme to arise from the London Gateway investigations. London was at the time the most important trading port in the world and the Thames Estuary was its vital artery.

A wide variety of sites were considered, from a fixed barrier against submarines, to the victims of the principal threats of mines and aerial bombing, to an aircraft that may have been involved in such bombing (Fig. 37). Some are highly unusual, such as one of the first ships to be sunk by an aircraft and some are related to unsung heroes of the conflicts such as the men of Trinity House. Many of the sites have additional significance to the themes considered above and it would be surprising if human remains were entirely absent.

All of the sites investigated are relevant to the Estuary's archaeological research framework, one of the objectives of which is to develop and understanding of defensive systems around the estuary and their role in relation to the estuary, London and South East England.

Late 19th- and 20th-century wrecks are very rarely studied archaeologically in the UK and the London Gateway project has thus allowed for the collection of data for potentially significant sites that, otherwise, are unlikely to have been recorded. Notwithstanding, the level of recording of these has been limited, and in most cases did not progress further than geophysical survey, because they were not considered important enough or because they were not eventually avoided by clearance. Diving investigations were however carried out if further clarification was required. It is the execution of this staged, systematic approach in a development-driven context which lies at the heart of the significance of the London Gateway investigations.

Aerial warfare against shipping in World War I and II

The use of aircraft in combat began during World War I. Although the technical limitations of early combat aircraft made flying over the sea difficult and hazardous, it quickly became apparent to both sides that shipping in the narrow confines of coastal waters and in the English Channel was vulnerable to aerial attack.

By 1915, the Germans had begun to attack Allied shipping both in the Channel and in the southern North Sea. However, the effectiveness of the aircraft available to both sides was very limited and it was not until 1917 that any Allied ships were sunk as a result of aerial attack. In that year the Germans managed to sink three ships through the use of torpedoes or the torpedo-bomb (Layman 2002, 91). In fact, throughout the war the aircraft achieved greater success in the reconnaissance and anti-submarine roles than in attack roles.

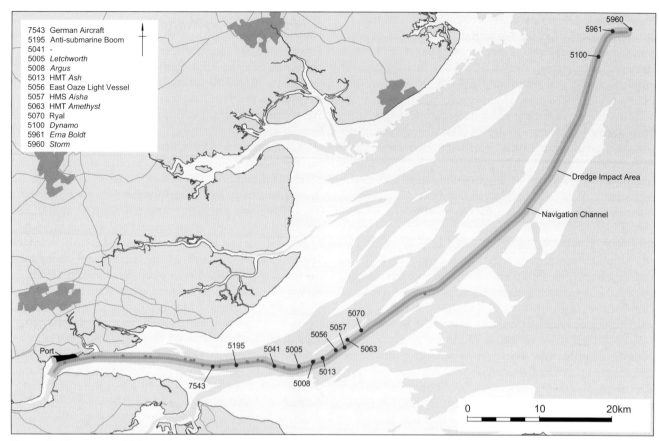

Figure 37: Location of World War I and II sites

By 1939 aircraft had become a much greater threat to shipping. The British relied upon coastal shipping for the distribution of bulk goods including food, raw materials and, crucially, the coal supply for the south-east and the south. The vital British coastal shipping fleet was therefore organised into convoys for defence. However, the fall of France, Belgium and Holland meant that the convoy routes in the southern North Sea and English Channel were close to Luftwaffe bases. As a result, until the Allies established air superiority in 1943, and the war in Russia and in the skies over Germany increasingly diverted the Axis air effort, these convoys were subject to intense air attack.

The Thames Estuary was both a destination and an assembly point, with Channel convoys bound for the naval base at Portsmouth, other south coast ports and further afield, and convoys heading to the north-east, assembling off Southend (Hewitt 2008, 23). Whilst the Estuary confines were relatively easy to defend against submarine and surface forces, it was highly vulnerable to air attack and the Luftwaffe was the principal threat, mounting attacks directly with torpedoes and bombs or, as the tide of war turned in 1942, increasingly by laying mines.

The southern North Sea and the Thames Estuary were also overflight zones, at first by Luftwaffe bombers, which used the Thames as an easily identifiable route to London during the Blitz and then by Allied bomber streams as an assembly area whilst flying to and from their targets on the continent. Accident and attack accounted for a significant number of aircraft losses over the Estuary.

Site 5960 (Storm)

(c 1.6km from the N edge of the dredged channel, close to the Storm Cardinal Buoy, c 26km off Harwich; depth 18.1m, Figs 37, 38)

The site lies outside the 2001 and 2002 survey areas but was targeted in 2006 multibeam survey undertaken by the PLA, and sidescan sonar survey undertaken in 2007. No diving investigations were carried out. The site lies inside the dredged impact area and will be subject to clearance. The site was rated as of 'possible' archaeological interest as there was only limited knowledge about the vessel's character and importance. No further archaeological mitigation was carried out.

The merchant steamship Storm was one of the first casualties of the use of aircraft at sea. It was a 55m long, 440 registered ton, iron screw-driven vessel, powered by a compound expansion engine and a single boiler. Originally built as SS Rosa by the Goole Engineering and Shipbuilding Company Ltd in 1875, it was a fine example of an early Goole steamer. In use as a collier on its last voyage, the ship is likely to have been operated as a tramp.

On 9 September 1917 Storm was on passage from Newcastle-upon-Tyne to Dunkirk with a cargo of coke when it was torpedoed and sunk by a German seaplane. Two members of the crew were lost. The ship appears to have been the victim of the German torpedo plane offensive of 1917. The wreck was reported to have been dispersed the following year.

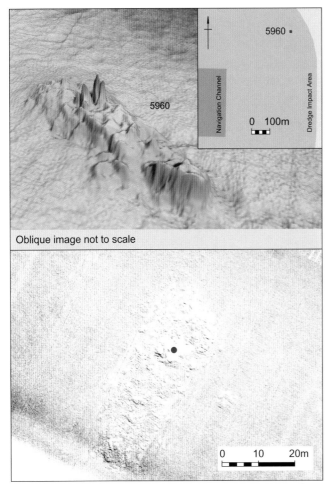

Figure 38: Multibeam bathymetry and sidescan images of Site 5960, *Storm*

Repeated surveys indicate that it remained a substantial wreck, although diving inspection in 1995 reported it in a poor state with old fishing nets snagged on it. In 2003 it was described as well broken up and buried (UKHO 14563: 12/8/2003). However, archaeological interpretation of the sidescan sonar and multibeam data acquired for London Gateway in 2007 (Fig. 38) identified a wreck that was at least partially intact.

The hull appeared to be sitting on an even keel and largely buried with the bow to the south-west. The anomaly was 56m long, suggesting that the full length of the hull survived. The minimum width was about 12m, suggesting some lateral break-up of the upper hull. Comparison with available photographs of the vessel suggested that elements of the superstructure were also present. A high point in the bathymetry suggested that although broken up, wreckage of the bridge and funnel aft of amidships was present. Some debris appeared to be scattered around the wreck. The location of the torpedo strike was not readily apparent.

Although no further archaeological investigation has been carried out, the scheme has successfully demonstrated the presence of substantial remains of a typical small steamship engaged in the home trade and a very early victim of the use of aviation against shipping. As noted elsewhere, whilst such wrecks are not uncommon, they are very rarely studied archaeologically.

Site 5005 (*Letchworth*)

(Seaward of Sea Reach 1, *c* 12km off Foulness; depth 16m, Figs 37, 39)

Site 5005 was not seen in 2001 sidescan sonar data and the coverage of the 2002 data did not extend to this section of the channel. A multibeam survey was carried out in 2005 and the site was dived by the PLA with Wessex Archaeology in 2006. The site was resurveyed with sidescan sonar survey in 2007. Changes to navigation, including the positioning of channel marker buoys adjacent to the site, meant that the site was to be avoided during dredging operations.

The loss of the *Letchworth* was the result of the considerable effort made by the Germans to disrupt the vital coastal trade of the East Coast and Thames Estuary during World War II.

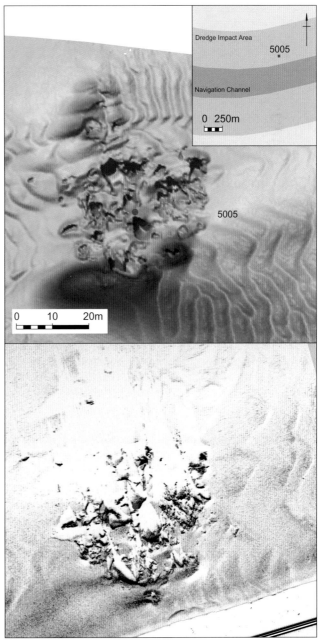

Figure 39: Multibeam bathymetry and sidescan images of Site 5005, *Letchworth*

Figure 40: Photograph of the SS *Letchworth*

Letchworth was built for the Watergate Steam Shipping Company Ltd in September 1924 by Wood Skinner and Company of Newcastle. Approximately 77m long, 1317 gross tons and powered by a triple expansion steam engine, it appears to have been a very typical collier of the inter-war years. The ship was engaged from 1925 in the London coal trade, bringing coal from the North-East to the capital (MacRae and Waine 1990; Talbot-Booth 1940). A number of plans and photographs of the *Letchworth* survive (Fig. 40).

Bound for London from Blyth, the convoy containing the *Letchworth* was intercepted by dive bombers on 1 November 1940 as it entered the Thames Estuary. An Admiralty Salvage Officer on board the vessel *King Lear* described the loss of the *Letchworth* as follows:

'At 2.30pm after clearing wreck (of *Houston City*) 10 to 12 enemy planes made dive bombing attack on wreck and ships in vicinity. S.S *Letchworth* of Newcastle 1317 tons, astern of *King Lear* sustained direct hit in engine room sinking immediately one cable's length E.S.E West Oaze Buoy. Bow portion bottom upwards still showing. Picked up 12 survivors including master, mate, and second mate. Five survivors picked up by S.S. *Hundvaag* of Stavanger. One member of crew, presumed to be chief engineer believed missing. All survivors transferred to Southend Lifeboat.'(TNA ADM 267/113).

The *Letchworth* seems to have rolled over as it sank. This attack was carried out by a Ju 87 Stuka divebomber. The raid may well have been the first in a series of daylight raids by Luftwaffe Stuka units against British shipping in the first half of November 1940 (Weal 2000, 83–6). These mass raids did not continue. Although the summer of 1940 was the worst period that the coastal convoys were to endure, with 234 losses (Hewitt 2008, 110), the failure of the Luftwaffe to win the Battle of Britain and the establishment of Allied air superiority in home waters meant that the aerial threat to coastal shipping gradually diminished as the war progressed.

No evidence has been traced that the Letchworth was subsequently dispersed as a dangerous wreck and it remained an easily located wreck in subsequent hydrographic surveys. Archaeological assessment of multibeam and sidescan sonar data acquired for London Gateway suggested that the wreck was fairly well broken up, with debris covering an area of 1350 square metres. The length of the anomaly, about 45m, was considerably shorter than the length of the ship and the south-west end of the wreck may have been buried (Fig. 39).

Subsequent archaeological diving inspection confirmed that the exposed portion of the wreck was partially broken up. Steel structure, including hull plating and frames was observed. In some places the structure of the vessel was intact and standing up to 3m high from the seabed. Other features located included a circular steel structure, possibly a boiler. There was much confused debris and broken and buckled plating and frames. This is suggestive of catastrophic damage to the vessel, either as a result of the bomb damage and the sinking or any subsequent clearance that may have taken place.

Further archaeological diving investigation was considered unlikely to be effective in adding to the information available through documentary research so, as the site was to be avoided during dredging operation, no further archaeological work was carried out. As with *Storm*, the scheme has successfully demonstrated the survival of a steamship, typical of the period in terms of use and build. The opportunities for diving the *Letchworth*, however, in conjunction with geophysical survey and documentary research, helped to establish the character and importance of the wreck to a greater extent.

Site 7543 (German Aircraft)

(200m south-east of Sea Reach 3, *c* 4km off Shoeburyness; depth 12.15m, Figs 37, 41)

The site was first discovered during the review of London Gateway sidescan sonar data acquired in 2001. It was also seen in the 2002 sidescan sonar investigations and in multibeam survey in 2006. The site was dived by the PLA in 2006 and again with Wessex Archaeology the same year.

In 2006 the PLA recovered part of a gearbox or tachometer drive, a gearwheel and an engine. The engine, retrieved from Site 7543 just within the southern edge of the channel, was identified as a Jumo 211. The site was first identified during the sidescan sonar survey undertaken for London Gateway in 2001 and further sidescan sonar and multibeam surveys indicated a cluster of small anomalies (Fig. 41).

The engine was marked 'MZM H 544' on the crankcase (Fig. 42). It does not appear to have been attached to other wreckage and a coherent aircraft wreck has not been found. Although it is possible that a buried airframe existed in the vicinity, the site is more likely to be the debris from an aircraft that either broke up as it crashed or was subsequently dispersed by human impacts such as trawling.

The Jumo 211 was an inverted V-12 German aircraft engine (Fig. 42), similar to the Daimler-Benz Engines which were their principal competitors (de la Bédoyère 2000, 185). They were used throughout World War II in Heinkel HE 111 and Junkers Ju 88 bombers and Junkers Ju 87 Stuka dive bombers, and over 68,000 units were produced in all (Hirschel *et al.* 2001, 209). From 1937 to the middle of 1944, the production of the Jumo 211 was spread between factories in Magdeburg, Kothen, Leipzig, Stettin and Strassburg (Kay 2004, 134). The lettering found on the Jumo 211 from Site 7543 indicates that it was manufactured at the Madgeburg facility (Motorenbau Zweigwerk Magdeburg) (de la Bédoyère 2000, 116, fig. 58).

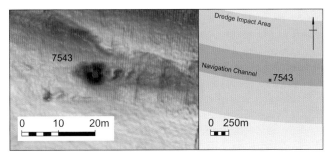

Figure 41: Multibeam bathymetry images of Site 7543, German Aircraft

Given that only a single engine was found, it has been suggested that the aircraft concerned was a single-engine Ju 87. Designed to work closely with the Wehrmacht, the German army, Stukas had been an important part of German 'Blitzkrieg' tactics, acting as a kind of highly mobile aerial artillery. They also had considerable success in the Mediterranean, severely damaging the aircraft carrier *Illustrious* (Winchester 2005, 146). Following the fall of France in June 1940 which enabled the Germans to use airbases just across the channel, heavy attacks were directed at allied shipping using Stukas.

However, they were slow and proved to be extremely vulnerable when faced with an organised fighter defence. During the Battle of Britain they were very roughly handled by the Hurricanes and Spitfires of the RAF and were withdrawn following the loss of 20% of their numbers in August 1940 (Ward 2004, 108–9).

The Stuka was used again briefly later in the same year for mass daylight attacks against shipping in the Thames and Straits of Dover. The *Letchworth* (5005) and the East Oaze Light Vessel (5056) were sunk during the first of these raids on 1 November and the Mouse Light Vessel, assisted subsequently by the *Argus* (5008), was repeatedly attacked in early November. Two minor Royal Navy vessels are also reported to have been sunk on 1 November and one Ju 87 was shot down, with one crew member lost and the other rescued by a Royal

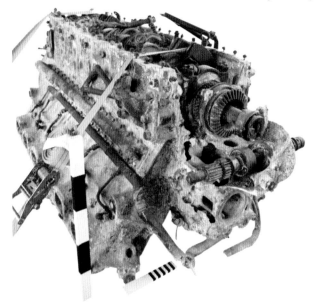

Figure 42: The Jumo 211 aircraft engine from Site 7543, which probably came from a Junkers 87

Navy torpedo boat (Weal 2000, 83). The recorded position of this loss (NRHE TQ 98 SW 166) is less than 1km from Site 7543.

Further raids against shipping by Stukas continued over the winter, resulting in the loss of the merchant ship SS *Astrologer*. However, the Stuka squadrons suffered heavy losses and in February 1941 they were retired from daylight raids and switched to night bombing runs during the London Blitz. The last reported loss was on the night of 12 February 1941, when a Ju 87 failed to return from a night sortie over the Thames Estuary (*ibid.*, 86).

It is not known whether the aircraft was intact when it crashed or if substantial break up may have resulted in the wide distribution of wreckage, as is common for aircraft crashing into the sea at speed. It is possible, therefore that the engine may have come from a twin-engine Ju 88 or Heinkel He 111 and that the second engine lies some distance away. Neither the geophysical survey nor diving investigations undertaken for London Gateway revealed any further material at the site. It may also be possible that any further aircraft wreckage may have been previously cleared from the site. In the absence of other identification evidence, the site remains a record of a German aircraft crash site but is otherwise a mystery.

Nonetheless, if the crash site is a Stuka, perhaps even the one lost on the 1 November in the raid that claimed the *Letchworth*, London Gateway's investigations have encapsulated both hunter and hunted in the air war against shipping, which was a critical element of World War II around the English Coast. The maritime recording of aviation wrecks is a specific area of research identified by the *Greater Thames Estuary Environment Research Framework* and the investigation of 7543 represents a very rare contribution to this and an opportunity to examine the previously uncharted loss of a German aircraft.

Site 5041 (Unknown Aircraft)

(Seaward of Sea Reach 1; 13.1m, Fig. 37)

The site was first identified in 1992 when fisherman reported a length of fuselage. The obstruction was not found during PLA surveys in 1991 and 1998 even though it was found through echo sounder in 1992. Neither the 2001 nor the 2002 sidescan sonar surveys for London Gateway located the obstruction and multibeam specifically focusing on site 5041 also failed to locate any remains. The site was cleared without the need for further mitigation.

A 40ft length of aircraft fuselage was located by a fisherman's snag in 1992. The PLA located a feature on the echo sounder later in the same year (it was not dived), and the obstruction has not been located since. It is unclear how the fisherman identified the obstruction as fuselage unless it was lifted, although there are no recorded reports of salvage or clearance works on the site since its discovery in 1992.

As the site was not found no further mitigation was required before clearance.

The U-Boat threat

German submarines had considerable success against coastal shipping on the east coast and in the approaches to the Thames Estuary in both world wars, by direct attack and by laying mines. In World War I they threatened to choke the supply of coal from the North East to London, until the institution of the convoy system and effective anti-submarine warfare equipment, but seem to have had relatively little success in penetrating the inner estuary.

During World War II submarines again struggled to penetrate the inner estuary due to the rapid construction of an anti-submarine boom and the intensive defence mounted by the Allies. The restricted navigation of the Estuary, and the difficulty of remaining on the surface without being observed, meant the main threat to Allied shipping came from the air. It is therefore not surprising that the only merchant ship investigated during the London Gateway project that was sunk by a submarine was lost during World War I in the approaches to the Estuary off Harwich.

Site 5961 (*Erna Boldt*)

(*c* 2km north-east of Sunk Light Vessel, *c* 25km off Harwich; depth 20.8m, Figs 37, 43)

The site was located outside the 2001 and 2002 survey areas but was targeted in the 2006 multibeam survey undertaken by the PLA. Sidescan sonar survey of the site was undertaken in 2007. No diving investigations were carried out and no further mitigation was required before clearance.

Erna Boldt was a screw-driven steel built merchant steamship, equipped with a triple expansion engine. Over 79m long and 1731 gross tons, the ship was built in 1908 by the *Neptun Schiffswerft und Maschinenfabrik Aktiengesellschaft* in Rostock, Germany. This was a major shipyard at the time, founded in 1850, and which launched the first German screw steamer, the *Erbgroßherzog Friedrich Franz*, in 1851. The company is still in operation today, having built over 1500 ships, and is now known as *Neptun Werft GmbH* (Stahl 1995).

The *Erna Boldt* was taken as an Admiralty prize and assigned to the management of Everett & Newbigin of Newcastle. It was carrying a cargo of coal from Newcastle-upon-Tyne to London on 9 September 1915 when it was torpedoed and sunk by the German submarine UC-11, a coastal minelaying submarine which sank 27 vessels until sunk itself in the Dover Straits after detonating a mine. The *Erna Boldt* is reported to have been sunk without warning. At the start of the war the rules concerning the engagement of merchant ships required them to be stopped, but as the war progressed ships started to be attacked without warning.

The wreck was partly dispersed in 1932. Thereafter, periodic hydrographic surveys continued to detect the

Figure 43: Multibeam bathymetry images of Site 5961, *Erna Boldt*

wreck, although its dimensions varied quite significantly, suggesting that it may have been partly buried at times. The sidescan sonar and multibeam surveys in 2006–7 revealed a substantial ship-shaped anomaly of 77–85m length (Fig. 43). The wreck was partially buried by sand waves at its south-western end. The highest points of the wreck were clustered in the centre of the site and almost 5m high. This may be the remains of a central island with bridge and funnel. The sidescan sonar data suggests that the wreck is breaking up.

The identification of this wreck as the *Erna Boldt* has previously been the subject of some uncertainty. However, the length of the wreck is a good match for the length of the ship and a correct identification therefore seems likely.

The *Erna Boldt* is unusual due to the combination of three factors: Firstly it was a prize vessel; secondly it was sunk by a torpedo, and; thirdly, the torpedo was launched by a submarine. The London Gateway investigations have confirmed its identity and have indicated that much remains, but its investigation will require diving if the wreck's potential to produce rare archaeological data concerning medium sized commercial steamships of the early 20th century is to be realised.

Site 5195 (Anti-submarine Boom)

(1.5km NE of the Great Nore Anchorage, 5km SE of Shoeburyness, Figs 37, 44)

Site 5195 was first located in 1981 during routine channel surveys and later that year divers recovered a section of wartime anti-submarine boom. The site was not identified during the 2001 sidescan sonar survey but was seen the 2002 sidescan and 2005 multibeam surveys along with nine further anomalies. No archaeological diving inspection was subsequently undertaken. Of the ten sites, those within, or close to, the channel were to be recovered. Limited archaeological observation and recording was carried out after recovery of the material within the footprint of the channel. Material outside of the channel will remain *in situ*.

The anti-submarine boom is represented by ten geophysical anomalies, scattered for *c* 200m along an approximate NS line across the river-bed. The boom was constructed in 1939–40 by the Admiralty between Shoeburyness and Minster.

The London Gateway surveys revealed ridges and both linear and block-like features, consistent with typical submarine boom debris composed of sinkers and cables for carrying netting (Fig. 44) (Wessex Archaeology 2008e).

The requirement for booms to guard against submerged vessels and torpedoes became apparent in World War I. It was further developed as the Royal Navy prepared for war in the late 1930s. Between 1938 and 1939 the submarine HMS *Seawolf* was involved in testing various designs in what became known as the 'Seawolf trials'. The importance of this work became even more apparent when the loss of the *Royal Oak* in 1939 at Scapa Flow exposed the vulnerability of otherwise heavily defended harbours to submarine attack.

The Admiralty decided to construct a defence boom in the Thames between Shoeburyness and the Isle of Sheppey. This was the first point where the deep water channels running from the outer estuary converge, and, at this location, the boom would also serve the Medway (TNA ADM/1/18128, 10/2/44).

The boom comprised three main components. In the shallow areas a fixed permanent structure piled into the seabed was constructed. In the deeper sections, which were navigable by large vessels and possibly submerged craft, a floating boom with netting was put in place. Finally, floating gate sections, also with netting, were placed in several positions along the deeper sections of the boom to allow vessels to pass through (Fig. 45).

The shallow water structure comprised a staggered row of wooden piles that extended from above the mean high water mark out into the river, over the sandbanks to a depth of approximately zero metres Chart Datum, where it was connected to the floating section. The piles protruded approximately 3.33m above the estuary bed. Sections of heavy-gauge angle iron were placed in between the tops of the piles to form a barrier.

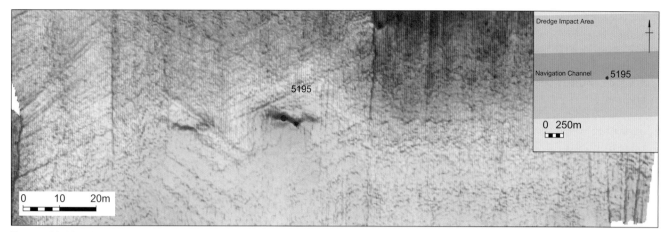

Figure 44: Multibeam bathymetry image of Site 5195, Anti-submarine Boom

The floating sections comprised a double layer of 'nets' constructed of steel mesh sections hung from surface cables between barges known as lighters. The surface cables were fitted with a double layer of cross shaped spikes to entrap vessels attempting to run through the defence. The ends of the surface sections were attached to fixed anchor points or a boat to hold them in place. They were secured to the riverbed by chain to large weights, known as sinkers.

The opening sections of the boom, known as gates, were constructed in the same way as the floating sections but were smaller in size and could be disconnected from the main boom and pulled to one side by a surface vessel, creating an opening in the defence. There were three gates: two to allow access to the Thames and one gate to the south to allow access to the Medway. They were operated by specialist boom vessels, stationed on either side, the whole structure being serviced by a variety of other small craft.

The PLA had located three of the anomalies in 1981 and the remains of the floating sections of the boom including chain with the surface spikes attached were recovered. Ground tackle used to secure the net to the bed, including a concrete sinker with fragments of steel cladding and chain attached and a series of concrete blocks chained together, were also recovered.

The boom was partially dismantled after the war and the floating sections were put into storage. The permanent structures were kept in place, should the boom need to be redeployed. In the 1950s, in the early years of the Cold War, the structure was upgraded. The wooden piles were replaced with concrete and the boom

was realigned to stretch from Shoeburyness to Sheerness. It was later demolished, apart from a 2km section just north of Shoebury East Beach, which is now a Scheduled Monument and which is believed to be a unique Cold War design (NRHE TQ 98 SE 131).

These remains are of archaeological interest as part of a massive defensive structure that crossed the entire Estuary. The appreciation of 20th-century military monuments as an important part of our archaeological heritage has increased in the last 20 years. This has led to initiatives such as the *Defence of Britain Project* of 1995–2002, which recorded a number of boom defence sites (but not the Thames boom). The importance of 20th-century military defence structures is also recognised by the regional research framework.

The work undertaken for London Gateway can be seen as a first step in the recording of what remains of this boom across the whole Estuary. Elements of this structure survive at Shoeburyness, and are also likely to survive at other locations across the estuary. Anti-submarine booms were installed across several other estuaries and port entrances around the world in World War II, and other examples are likely to survive. There is considerable heritage interest in defensive structures from World War II, including amongst local and national heritage agencies as well as the population at large.

Site 5063 (HMT *Amethyst*)

(Seaward of Sea Reach 1, Oaze Deep, *c* 12km SE of Foulness; depth 16.5m, Figs 37, 46)

The site was located outside the 2001 and 2002 survey areas but was targeted in the 2005 multibeam survey undertaken by the PLA. Sidescan sonar survey of the site was undertaken in 2007. No diving investigations were carried out. No further archaeological investigation has taken place as the site lies outside the navigation channel and will be avoided by clearance activities.

Site 5063 is the remains of HMT *Amethyst*, one of 15 trawlers known as the Gem Group purchased by the Admiralty in 1935 and 1939 and converted for anti-submarine defence.

Figure 45: Submarine boom in place

Amethyst was built as the steam trawler *Phyllis Rosalie* (Fig. 47) for the Boston Deep Sea Fishing and Ice Co Ltd of Fleetwood by Smith's Dock Co Ltd, Middlesbrough in 1934 (Lloyd's Register). It was 47.9m long, steel built and 433 gross tons. In its first year it made the port's best single trip landing and went on to beat its own record the following year. The trawler represented Fleetwood at the King George V Silver Jubilee Spithead Review and the skipper, Mr W. Holmes, was presented to the King (FLOAT 2010). In November 1935 as Britain began to rearm, the vessel was purchased by the Admiralty, renamed *Amethyst*, and converted for anti-submarine service. It was fitted with ASDIC and armed with a single four-inch gun on the bow and depth charges at the stern.

According to logbook entries (TNA ADM 53/94739 and ADM 53/101095), the vessel was mainly occupied with fleet and anti-submarine exercises before it became a tender to the submarine depot ship *Cochrane* in Rosyth in 1939. In 1940 *Amethyst* reportedly took part in the Dunkirk operation. In November of that year it sank after reportedly detonating one of the early versions of the acoustic mine in the Barrow Deep. Blown up at the stern, the trawler took about ten minutes to sink. The crew, including seven wounded men were picked up

Figure 47: The trawler *Phyllis Rosalie* before conversion for anti-submarine defence as HMT *Amethyst*

by the trawler *Le Tiger* and taken to Southend Pier, where they were apparently taken in charge by suspicious police who had earlier arrested the crew of a Dutch vessel which had also been mined (Lund and Ludlam 1971).

The wreck, which is about 90m north of the channel, was initially marked with a buoy but then dispersed in 1941. Archaeological assessment of the multibeam and sidescan sonar data collected for London Gateway revealed a ship-shaped anomaly 50m long, which approximates to the original length of the vessel (Fig. 46). The *Amethyst* was upright and lying on a north-north-west to south-south-east axis. The hull appeared to be largely buried (possibly enveloped by a sandbank) with what appears to be the bow to the south, surrounded by a deep scour. The hull also appeared to be largely intact and its profile approximated that of the original vessel. It was covered with the remains of collapsed superstructure and deck fittings. There was some lateral spread of debris amidships, together with a large upstanding feature that may be the remains of the funnel.

The site has not been cleared and no archaeological diving investigation was mounted following the geophysical survey. As a result it is not possible to confirm whether the geophysical interpretation is correct. Nevertheless, the *Amethyst* has similar importance to the *Ash* described below. Although the investigation has been limited by the lack of diving involvement, it does represent a rare attempt to record a class of vessel that has received no significant archaeological attention previously.

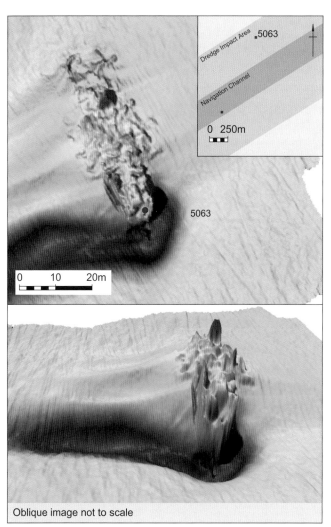

Figure 46: Multibeam bathymetry image of Site 5063, HMT *Amethyst*

Patrol craft, mines and minesweepers

The fall of France, Norway and the Netherlands in 1940 meant that the south and east coasts of England became the frontline in the fight against Hitler's Germany. The Thames Estuary, as the gateway to the capital, became an important battlefield as the Royal Navy and Air Force sought to both defend the vital coastal trade and prevent invasion.

Within easy range of Luftwaffe bases on the continent and with no sea room to manoeuvre, the Estuary was too vulnerable to act as a base for the Navy's capital ships. Instead, it was defended throughout the war by a range of small craft of the Royal Naval Patrol Service (RNPS), Coastal Forces and the Royal Navy's general service.

Founded in 1939 but with origins dating back to 1907, the Patrol Service's role was to minesweep and hunt submarines in coastal waters, principally around harbours. In the inter-war period it was a part-time force of fishermen. Starting in 1939 with an initial fleet comprising 6,000 fishermen and 200 requisitioned trawlers, drifters, pleasure steamers and whaling vessels, it expanded to a force of 60,000 men in about 3,000 small vessels (TNA ADM 1/9936). The Patrol Service was spread around the ports of the United Kingdom, including the Thames Estuary and abroad but its main base was Lowestoft, chosen principally because it was a major centre of the fishing industry and because it was close to the Thames Estuary (Lavery 2006, 256).

Disparagingly known to the general service as 'Harry Tate's Navy', serving in the Patrol Service was hazardous and the service suffered more than 3,000 casualties, most of whom were 'missing, presumed dead'. In addition to minesweeping and submarine hunting, the RNPS also undertook convoy escort, harbour and boom defence and some of the work of the Examination Service, which inspected civilian vessels arriving in British waters.

Patrol Service vessels were most commonly trawlers. These were mainly requisitioned deep sea fishing trawlers, as they were designed for towing equipment through the water and could be adapted easily. The larger trawlers could also be used for convoy escort. However, these trawlers often had too deep a draught for inshore work and purpose-designed 'Admiralty trawlers' had to be built for this role. In addition, a wide range of other requisitioned craft was used, including drifters and yachts. The latter ranged in size from large motor yachts, such as the submarine tender *Cutty Sark* of 884 tons, to small vessels with a crew of only five or six (*ibid.*, 255). In total, about 1700 civilian vessels were requisitioned during the war.

The mines laid by German aircraft, submarines and patrol vessels were the greatest threat to coastal shipping during World War II. Mines were the commonest cause of loss of British warships, particularly of smaller vessels which were often blown apart with no survivors if they hit a mine (HMSO 1947, 40–1).

Mines were a particular danger in the restricted navigation of the Estuary, where they were often delivered by air. As a result, large numbers of minesweepers were based in and around the Thames Estuary, for example at Queenborough on the Swale. Purpose built minesweepers had been given a very low priority by the Admiralty before the war but, as it progressed, various types were built to supplement, and then replace, the requisitioned vessels that had undertaken most of the work in the early war years and which had proved highly vulnerable, particularly to magnetic mines. The new vessels included

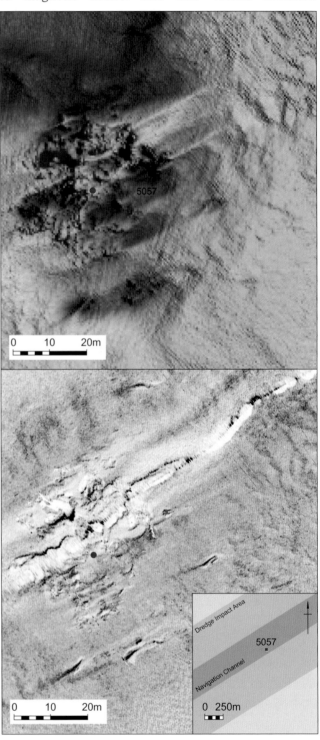

Figure 48: Multibeam bathymetry and sidescan images of Site 5057, *Aisha*

Admiralty trawlers and motor minesweepers optimised for short-range harbour and estuary clearance. They used diesel engines and wooden hulls that reduced their magnetic signature.

A review of NRHE records of both requisitioned fishing and mine warfare vessels wrecks indicates that, although they are fairly common, they only appear to have been examined archaeologically in the context of the London Gateway investigations (Wessex Archaeology 2011c, 28 and 52–3). The examination of four wrecks engaged in or lost as a consequence of mine warfare and coastal defence (including the *Amethyst* (5063) above) therefore appears to represent the first serious attempt to record this important aspect of our naval archaeology in the inshore waters of England.

Site 5057 (HMS *Aisha*)

(Oaze Deep, *c* 13km off Foulness Island; depth 18.2m, Figs 37, 48)

The site was located outside the 2001 and 2002 survey areas but was seen in the multibeam and sidescan sonar survey undertaken in 2008. No diving investigations were carried out and no further mitigation was required before clearance.

The *Aisha* was a 30m long, 117 gross ton steel motor yacht, originally built as the *Wilna* in Selby, Yorkshire in 1934. Until 1938 it was owned by William H. Collins of Slough, Buckinghamshire. The *Wilna* was purchased in 1939 by Robert H. Turner of Guildford, Surrey and, in 1940, was hired as a Harbour Defence Patrol Craft and renamed (Colledge 1989, 18). The vessel was refitted and armed with a gun mounted on the foredeck.

Our knowledge of what *Aisha* looked like is based upon a surviving model of the ship in civilian guise (Fig. 49) and a photograph in wartime service (web accessed). Little documentary evidence for the vessel's career has been traced. The son of one of *Aisha's* wartime crew members confirms that it took part in the Dunkirk evacuation of 1940 (D. Fletcher, pers. comm.).

Aisha was lost after hitting a mine in the Thames Estuary on 11 October 1940 (D. Fletcher, pers. comm.). Exactly why the vessel was there has not been established. The descendant of another crew member recalls that, after being damaged at the stern, *Aisha* was taken in tow by a destroyer but slowly sank (J. Knill, pers. comm.).

Archaeological assessment of the surveys carried out in 2008 by the PLA revealed that the wreck was broken up and scattered over an area of about 1800 square metres (Fig. 48). This is consistent with UKHO records that it had been fairly comprehensively dispersed, probably using explosives, by 1946 (UKHO 14062, report 26/6/1946). No further archaeological recording of *Aisha* was carried out for London Gateway.

Site 5013 (HMT *Ash*)

(Oaze Deep, *c* 12.5km off Foulness Island; depth 16.5m, Figs 37, 50)

The site was located outside the 2001 and 2002 survey areas but was seen in multibeam and sidescan sonar survey undertaken in 2005 and 2007 respectively. No diving investigations were carried out and no further mitigation was required before clearance.

The 530 ton, 50m long HMT *Ash* was one of 20 wooden Tree Class Admiralty trawlers built during World War II for minesweeping duties. It was built by Cochrane and Sons, who had a long history of building trawlers for the Admiralty, in Selby in 1939 and the engine was built by Amos and Smith (Toghill 2003). Equipped with a single shaft reciprocating steam engine, which delivered 850 horsepower, the *Ash* was capable of a top speed of 11.5 knots. The trawler was armed with a single 12-pounder gun at the bow, together with various anti-aircraft guns including Lewis and Hotchkiss machine guns. It would have been crewed by 35 men (Cocker 1993).

Ash had a busy and distinguished early war service and had swept for 18 channel convoys by 1941. Second Hand K.R. Lazenby, RNPS, X.7590C was awarded the

Figure 49: Scale model of *Wilna*, later renamed *Aisha*

Distinguished Service Medal and Lieutenant A.G. Newell, NZRNVR, commanding officer and Engineman L. Elton, KX.98260 were mentioned in despatches for courage and continuous good service with the channel convoys (TNA ADM 1/11651).

However, on 6 June 1941 the ship's luck ran out. Proceeding with the trawler *Birch* ahead of convoy C.W.3Y, in order to carry out minesweeping between Shingles and Dumpton at the mouth of the Thames Estuary, the ship detonated a mine (TNA ADM 1/11295). The explosion occurred abaft of midships on the starboard side, causing the vessel to start flooding. The *Birch* came alongside and transferred publications and charts, the Lewis and Hotchkiss guns, small arms and all ammunition, as well as some of the ship's fittings including compasses and signal lamps, for example, and personal effects. *Ash* was then taken into tow and both trawlers set course for Sheerness but the *Ash* sank *en route*.

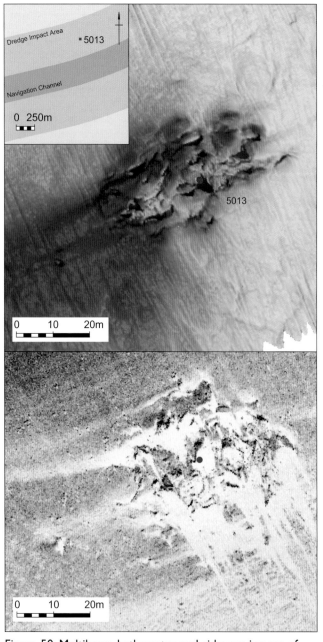

Figure 50: Multibeam bathymetry and sidescan images of Site 5013, HMT *Ash*

The wreck, which lay just to the north of the channel, was dispersed by the Royal Navy in 1942 and was thereafter the subject of hydrographic survey at intervals. Archaeological assessment of multibeam (Fig. 50) and sidescan sonar surveys carried out for London Gateway located an area of debris covering an area of approximately 1500 square metres, with debris at a height of up to 2.5m above the seabed. It was concluded that the wreck was well broken up. As with *Aisha*, no further pre-clearance archaeological recording of HMT *Ash* was carried out for London Gateway.

The investigation of *Ash* and *Aisha* (and the *Amethyst* considered in the previous section), although based only upon geophysical survey, is significant as it appears to be the first time that either a harbour patrol craft or an Admiralty trawler of World War II has been examined and recorded in a planned manner at sea. Whilst the data produced has been limited, it demonstrates recognition that unspectacular, but nevertheless potentially significant, wrecks of this type and period nevertheless warrant archaeological investigation and recording. *Ash*, *Aisha* and *Amethyst* (and *Dynamo* and the MV *Ryal* described below) were all lost to mines and they are a very vivid archaeological reminder of the dangers posed to small coastal defence vessels by mines.

Site 5070 (MV *Ryal*)

(*c* 1 mile SW of Knob Light Vessel seaward of Sea Reach No. 1; 19m, Fig. 37)

Site 5070 and a further anomaly (7209) were seen in the 2001 sidescan sonar survey and a multibeam survey carried out in 2005. Both lay outside the coverage of the 2002 sidescan data. No diving investigations were carried out. No further archaeological investigation has taken place as the site lies outside the dredged channel and will be avoided by clearance activities.

The MV *Ryal* was lost on the 21 November 1941 after hitting a mine one mile south-west of the Knob Light Vessel. The vessel was lost whilst *en route* to Middlesbrough carrying a cargo of 350 tonnes of steel. Nine members of the crew perished as a result of the sinking.

The wreck was first dispersed in September 1945 to a depth of 13.72m, it was then drift swept to a depth of 14m in October 1945. The wreck was further drift swept in 1954 to a depth of 14.62m. The site was surveyed again in 1973, 1990, 2001 and 2005 but no further clearance work was carried out. Despite this early clearance the sidescan sonar and multibeam surveys showed extensive and coherent remains.

The 2002 sidescan showed Site 5070 as an anomaly 20m long by 25m wide. Site 7209 consisted of a 2m by 2m anomaly 10m to the north and was identified as debris associated with the wreck. The multibeam shows Site 5070 emerging from the edge of a sandbank that demarks the topographic edge of the shipping channel, which may indicate further debris may exist on the upper edge of the sandbank. The wreck is rectangular in shape and orientated north-east, south-west. It is 45m long by 20m wide and is 3m upstanding on the north-eastern end.

It is possible that the site contains important evidence for wartime vessels, which could contribute to our understanding of life on board at the time of loss, and for changes in structure and design relevant to use in wartime. Further documentary research into its home port of Newcastle could reveal details of its history. However, as this site will be avoided, its potential to inform has been preserved.

Site 5100 (*Dynamo*)

(*c* 21km off the Naze, near Harwich, Fig. 37)

As the location and investigation methods for this site are described in detail above and illustrated (Fig. 34), they are not repeated here. These methods included multibeam and sidescan sonar surveys; no diving was undertaken.

The 809 gross ton, 56m long *Dynamo* (see above) has already been considered in the context of late 19th- and early 20th-century steamships. However, as a typical target and victim of the German mining campaign, it is worth mentioning here. Unfortunately, the impact of the mine that sank it is not apparent from the geophysical data (Fig. 35) and the site has not been dived. However, it is doubtful whether the diving investigations carried out for London Gateway would have been able to distinguish between explosive impacts that sank the vessel and those used to disperse the wreckage.

Trinity House at war

The role of Trinity House during World War II should not be underestimated. While the lights of many of Britain's lighthouses were extinguished for defensive reasons, the remaining lighthouses, navigation buoys and, in particular, light vessels remained to provide essential navigation aids for both merchant and naval ships. Trinity House pilots guided ships, including many casualties of enemy action, into Britain's ports. Trinity House vessels maintained a complex network of buoys marking the coastal convoy routes (Hewitt 2008, 39). Various support vessels and tenders also took to new duties, such as minesweeping, and participated in military operations, such as the evacuation of the Channel Islands and the D-Day landings. Trinity House vessels, particularly light ships, naturally became targets for enemy action. The wrecks of two of these vessels were investigated as part of the London Gateway project.

Site 5056 (East Oaze Light Vessel)

(East of Sea Reach 1, Oaze Deep, *c* 12.5km off Foulness Island; depth 21m, Figs 37, 51)

Site 5056 was located during the 2001 sidescan survey but was located outside the 2002 survey. In 2005 the PLA undertook a multibeam survey and diving investigations. Further sidescan sonar survey was carried out in 2007.

The East Oaze Light Vessel was built in 1888 by R. Stephenson and Co of Newcastle. This company was owned by the son of the famous railway engineer

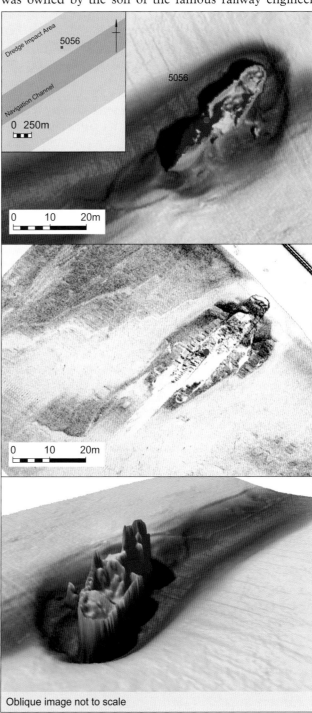

Figure 51: Multibeam bathymetry and sidescan images of Site 5056, the East Oaze Light Vessel

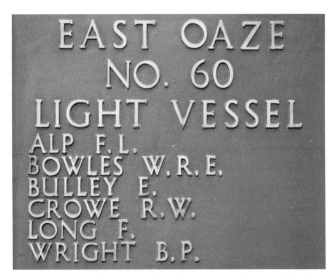

Figure 52: East Oaze Light Vessel tribute on Tower Hill Memorial

Robert Stephenson. It was designated Trinity House Light Vessel No. 60 and plans of its sister ship, Light Vessel No. 61, are still held in the Trinity House Archives. The light vessel was just over 31m long, 7m in the beam and 265 registered tons.

During World War II the vessel served as a 'port war signal station' – a light vessel positioned to control an entrance to a defensively mined entrance or to mark a safe passage through a minefield for coastal convoys making their way up the Thames Estuary. In this role it was sunk by German aircraft on 1 November 1940 with the loss of all six crew (Young 1989, 62).

Whilst there is no definitive information on the identity of the attacking aircraft, the 1 November saw a brief resumption in mass attacks upon shipping in the Estuary by Stuka dive bombers, an aircraft which was equipped with the type of Jumo 211 engine found at Site 7543. The Letchworth (5005) was sunk on the same day.

In 1948, the wreck was subject to Royal Navy dispersal operations, probably using explosives. It was surveyed at intervals, sidescan anomalies detected in 1998 being interpreted as in situ moorings. The London Gateway survey data showed a relatively intact wreck, lying upright and apparently on an even keel in a deep scour, with its bow to the south-west in the middle of the channel (Fig 51). The wreck measured c 40 x 12m; its highest point about 7.5m above the base of the deep scour that completely surrounded it. Part of the hull at the stern of the lightship was almost intact. Amidships and towards the bow the sides of the ship were not complete, though a number of structural features were also identifiable at the bow, including the possible remains of the ship's light derrick. A bulkhead was visible amidships. The sidescan sonar survey also revealed the remains of anchor chains at the bow and stern extending towards mooring blocks lying to the east and west of the wreck.

Diving inspection carried out by the PLA in 2005 broadly confirmed this interpretation and also observed snagged fishing gear, together with intact wooden fendering. The diver described the vessel as being of steel

construction. The vessel is recorded by Trinity House as being of composite construction, which is normally the description applied to vessels with iron frames and wooden planking and as the marine growth covering the wreck was heavy and the visibility nil, it may be that the fendering felt was in fact planking. Unfortunately a subsequent archaeological diving operation had to be aborted before inspection began and this question remained unresolved before clearance.

The description "composite" is often erroneously applied to ship hulls built using both metal and wood from all periods, but was, in fact, a fairly short-lived mid-19th-century form of ship construction based on iron frames with wooden planking that was thought to offer advantages in terms of anti-fouling and resistance to rot. Although it ultimately proved to be an unsuccessful compromise, it did briefly help rejuvenate the British shipbuilding industry in the 1860s (Slaven 1992, 2) and certain types of vessels designed for speed such as yachts continued to be built in this way into the 20th century. There are no references to composite hulls in the NRHE and it is believed to be very rare and unstudied feature of wrecks in UK territorial waters (Wessex Archaeology 2011a, 11–12).

The six crew of the East Oaze Light Vessel are commemorated by a plaque on the Tower Hill Memorial (Fig. 52).

Site 5008 (Argus)

(Seaward of Sea Reach 1, Oaze Deep, c 12km off Foulness Island; depth 16.5–19m, Figs 37, 53)

The site was located outside the 2001 and 2002 survey areas but was targeted in the 2005 multibeam survey undertaken by the PLA. Sidescan sonar survey of the site was undertaken in 2007. No diving investigations were carried out. The site will be avoided during dredging operations by changes to navigation, including the positioning of channel marker buoys adjacent to the site. No further archaeological mitigation is proposed.

The Argus was a 661 gross ton steamship, built for Trinity House as a tender or support vessel and the fourth (out of five) of that name. These vessels were used to service buoys and light vessels and during World War II they were all defensively armed due to the threat from German aircraft.

The 52m long Argus was built in 1909 by Ramage & Ferguson in Leith for the Corporation of Trinity House (Middlemiss 1995). Powered by a triple expansion steam engine driving twin screws, it was armed with either a 12-pounder quick firing gun or Lewis guns (Woodman 2005).

On 11 November 1940 Argus was despatched to salvage gear from the wreck of the Trinity House vessel Reculver, which had been mined off the mouth of the Humber. The ship was first to relieve the crew of the Mouse Light Vessel, which had been bombed by enemy aircraft several nights in a row, again reflecting the upsurge in an anti-shipping activity by the Luftwaffe in

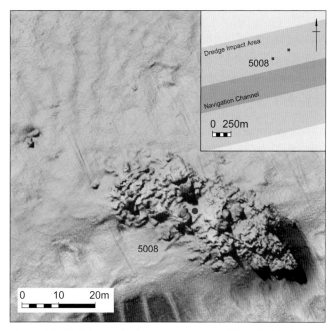

Figure 53: Multibeam bathymetry image of Site 5008, *Argus*

the Thames in early November 1940. The following day it had to remain at anchor until late afternoon until an easterly gale eased off and they were able to put the light vessel crew back onboard. Shortly after setting sail for Harwich, the vessel hit a mine. The following account of what happened is based on the direct testimony of the only survivor out of 35 crew (Woodman 2005):

"There was a sudden blinding flash. Quartermaster Smith was hurled into the corner of the wheelhouse where, dazed and semi-conscious, he reached instinctively for the wheel. It spun impotently in his hands. Eventually he stood up, a pain in his legs, staggered through what was left of the wheelhouse bulkhead and out on the bridge wing. He was dazed and totally at a loss what to do. He stared aft. *Argus* was down to her boat deck. Below him most of his 34 shipmates were already dead, immobilised by broken legs and pelvises and finally drowned. Suddenly he was joined by another man. The 2nd Officer, in pilot jacket and leather half boots, took one look aft and dived overboard. Smith followed his example, finding the water bitterly cold. He never saw the 2nd Officer again. Around him wreckage and dead fish filled his head with irrelevant regrets that he could not fry up some of the latter. Eventually he clambered, with great difficulty, on a carley float and lay half in the water, shivering with cold."

Smith was picked up by the anti-aircraft vessel *Royal Eagle* and spent the following three months in hospital. Soon after the loss a wreck buoy was laid at the site by the Trinity House vessel *Patricia*. The crew reported seeing the personal items of the lost crew floating to the surface, but no bodies were recovered (*ibid.*). The wreck was regarded as dangerous and dispersal operations

eventually took place in 1959. Thereafter periodic surveys reported a still substantial wreck.

Archaeological interpretation of the multibeam data acquired for London Gateway in 2005 showed that the wreck was still partially intact, sitting on its keel within a distinctive scour and about 89m north of the channel (Fig. 53). The wreck had a coherent shape and was approximately 60m long, with a surviving height of up to 4.5m in the scour at the south-east end, suggesting that most of the hull might survive. However, the decision was taken not to clear the site in view of its sensitivity as a war grave and no archaeological diving operation subsequently took place.

The work on the East Ouse Light Vessel and on the *Argus* carried out for London Gateway is thought to have been the first archaeological investigation of Trinity House vessels in the UK. Whilst the amount of information recorded was limited by the lack of archaeological diving operations, the project has contributed to the recording of the remains of such vessels at sea.

The remains of the 35 dead of the *Argus* are commemorated on the Tower Hill Memorial.

Figure 54: *Argus* tribute on Tower Hill Memorial

Discussion
A New Maritime Archaeology of the Thames Estuary?

OUTCOMES AND INNOVATIONS

The overriding success of the wetside archaeology programme was that consent was obtained and construction of London Gateway proceeded without archaeology becoming a 'scheme stopper', despite the undoubtedly sensitive character of the Thames. This might seem like a naive starting point; could archaeology really, seriously get in the way of a major port proposal? Whilst it is true that archaeology does not have the regulatory standing of some other environmental concerns – in terms of specific international and European levels of protection, administrative tenacity or NGO concern – but it is not entirely uncontentious. Procedural rules under EIA regulations are such that inadequate consideration of the archaeological heritage could impede consent, for example, and the restrictions that apply through statutory protection of specific sites could be a major problem to a developer if designation becomes the only mechanism available to curators. There is also quite a high level of public interest in wrecks and underwater archaeology, which can escalate into intractable objections from members of the public and local organisations if concerns are not addressed. Certainly, other major port schemes have faced circumstances where archaeology alone could have derailed otherwise steady progress towards consent.

London Gateway succeeded in safeguarding some important sites, especially the two sites forming the wreck of the *London* (Sites 5019/5029). Both sites were known well before the London Gateway investigations, and in fact it was a private salvage operation that led to designation under the *Protection of Wrecks Act* 1973. Throughout the EIA process the channel designs were such that the *London*/'King' and 'Iron Bar Wreck' would be directly impacted. Without input from marine archaeologists, and the conduct of higher resolution geophysical surveys at the instigation of archaeologists which gave a clearer indication of the extent of survival, it is likely that these wrecks would have been dispersed mechanically and subjected to dredging. Certainly, there had been few qualms about using high impact clearance methods on the 16th-century Gresham Ship in 2003 before its importance was acknowledged (Auer and Firth 2007). An estimate of the cost of archaeological mitigation on these sites in advance of dredging was a turning point. The outcome, however, was that the channel alignment was changed and the sites protected *in situ*, supported by explicit exclusion zones and provision for monitoring before, during and after dredging.

Other sites have also been protected *in situ*, not necessarily for solely archaeological reasons – avoidance of disturbing 'war graves' has been an important influence, as has been the cost of clearance – but the archaeological, historical and geophysical information brought to bear by archaeologists has certainly contributed to the context within which decisions have been made. Sites such as the *Argus* (5008), *Amethyst* (5063), and *Letchworth* (5005) have consequently been avoided or subject to minimal disturbance and will continue to survive as physical memorials to the 20th-century history of the Thames.

The project has demonstrated that reconsideration and redesign of proposed dredging and navigational works is a viable approach when dealing with the historic environment of ports. Despite the many, major constraints on the design of navigational channels and the enormous expense they may entail – and the costly inconvenience of redesign and reassessment – London Gateway has shown that this approach is worthwhile. Even if the presence of heritage assets is not the main driver, opportunities for mitigation by avoidance should certainly be sought. Aside from avoiding major impacts on *in situ* sites of national if not international significance, by moving the channel London Gateway also avoided the costs of intrusive mitigation. Even if highly selective, such mitigation would have been operationally complex and very costly. A lesson to take forward is that mitigation by avoidance could have been given greater consideration at an earlier stage of development, rather than after the EIA had been submitted.

An important area of cross-over between London Gateway and other forms of marine development-led archaeology has been in the introduction of protocols for archaeological discoveries made in the course of construction. Protocols emerged for port developments such as capital dredging in Belfast Lough and marine aggregate dredging in the late 1990s in order to reduce the need for watching briefs by archaeologists during extensive marine operations, placing responsibility – with archaeological support – on the staff engaged in construction. London Gateway was informed by this earlier work, and the introduction of a protocol was an attractive inclusion in the mitigation package. The contribution of London Gateway to the evolution of such protocols emerged once dredging had started, as it quickly became the most intense and prolific protocol implemented to date. The practical feedback to be gained about protocol implementation – including how to deal with large numbers of very varied archaeological objects, and how to respond to significant sites as they come to light – will be a major avenue through which London Gateway will influence archaeological practice in future.

The early adoption of a far-reaching Archaeological Mitigation Framework (AMF) that encompassed the entire scheme, informed by an explicit research perspective to inform decision-making, was another important facet of the London Gateway scheme. The AMF helped overcome some of the complexities created by the multiple consents that were required. The need for three different Environmental Statements certainly added to the already heavy demands of EIA for major infrastructure, but the AMF provided a single focal point for discussions and agreement between the developer, regulator, curators and archaeological consultants and contractors. Streamlining of consenting processes for nationally significant infrastructure projects and for marine licensing mean that the basic complexity of consenting and EIA should be less of an issue in future, but it remains the case that processes are facilitated by concise archaeological documentation.

The Clearance Mitigation Statements (CMSs) were a similarly innovative form of documentation, which again were central to discussions and agreements between the parties concerned with implementing consent. Each CMS brought together documentary, geophysical and archaeological evidence into a single account, framed in a way that elicited the key characteristics and importance of each site and provided a reasoned case for the form of mitigation being proposed. The CMS played an important role in transforming the mass of sites listed in gazetteers into individual heritage assets that had each to be considered in their own right as well as in terms of an assemblage brought together by the footprint of the scheme.

In terms of outputs, London Gateway is one of the first marine developments in the United Kingdom to be accompanied by a popular booklet, *London Gateway: a maritime history* (Wessex Archaeology 2010d) to inform the public of the archaeological processes and results that have underpinned the development. This monograph is also an important milestone, bearing in mind the small number of publications that explore the regulatory and methodological genesis of marine development-led projects as well as the archaeological results. Deposition of the archive with the local museum service of Southend-on-Sea is another important 'first' that is already providing valuable practical experience for the profession as a whole (Satchell 2012).

Methods and techniques

London Gateway has contributed to overall methodological development in many spheres of marine archaeology. The sequence of desk-based assessment, evaluation, mitigation and post-excavation analysis was developed for terrestrial archaeology and is widely practiced on development projects of various scales.

From the outset, London Gateway presented a relatively early case of this staged approach being applied to marine development. It subsequently became a still-rare example of a marine project progressing all the way from relatively common desk-based studies through different forms of field evaluation to pre-construction mitigation, including excavation and recovery of wreck material, accompanied by post-fieldwork provision for material conservation and archive deposition. Mitigation during construction – still underway at the time of writing – is to be published separately. London Gateway also introduced and demonstrated several elaborations of the staged approach. It presented an early example of area-wide geophysical survey being conducted and interpreted primarily for archaeological purposes in the course of the EIA. Geophysical survey was also used as a central method of field evaluation of individual sites. It also exhibited iterative stages of diving as a form of both non-intrusive and intrusive field evaluation, using both fully-archaeological and combined commercial-archaeological diving teams.

Looking at some of these stages individually, in relation to desk-based assessment subsequent experience has shown that the scope for useful sources of previous data could be expanded. Specifically, there are valuable documentary resources that have hitherto remained relatively obscure and unused in the context of maritime desk-based assessment, which have a bearing in particular on clarifying the presence, position and importance of coastal and other small vessels of the 19th and 20th centuries. Whilst it may not be cost-effective to examine these sources in the initial phase of assessment, detailed examination of primary documentary records may prove an efficient approach to dealing with uncertainties that might otherwise take up geophysical or diving resources.

The success of geophysical survey in relation to London Gateway was in providing a relatively rapid and cost-effective means of examining the footprint of the scheme for the presence of archaeological features. In the early 2000s there was no expectation that design or impact assessment of major dredging for a port would include comprehensive geophysical survey at an early stage; bathymetry – even single beam bathymetry – could suffice. This certainly contrasts with the approach that was already being taken to marine aggregate dredging and became standard practice for offshore renewable schemes in the same timeframe. In part this provided the motivation for archaeologically-directed geophysics, because it was only archaeologists that were pressing the case for sidescan sonar and magnetometer surveys to be carried out. In other marine development sectors the emphasis was not on carrying out expensive new surveys, but on ensuring that equivalent surveys for engineering or environmental purposes incorporated archaeological objectives in an integrated way, at little additional cost.

The 2002 sidescan sonar and magnetometer survey was a tremendous advantage to the EIA and to subsequent project planning and decision-making. However, not even archaeologically-designed survey specifications and specialist interpretation can explain every trace suspected as having an archaeological origin.

The interpretation of 'uncertains' is discussed in more detail below, but it is important to acknowledge here that as well as the things that can be 'seen' but not explained, geophysical survey cannot see everything. Sites that are buried and have no physical expression on the surface of the seabed are invisible to sidescan sonar (and bathymetric) survey, as are sites that have no ferrous content to magnetometers. Even where magnetic anomalies are observed for buried sites, little can be concluded about their origin or possible importance, nor are they an easy target for inspection by diver or ROV. These geophysical blind spots must be factored in to the discussion of archaeological potential and risk, because buried and/or non-magnetic material can encompass a very wide range of important heritage assets.

Another benefit of geophysical survey was its use in providing data on form and character that could be used directly in assessing and evaluating sites, as well as simply establishing presence and position. High-resolution geophysics also provided base mapping for further investigation by diving and for longer-term needs such as the archaeological monitoring of clearance operations. The efficiency of later phases of investigations and decision-making would have been seriously compromised had geophysical data not been available.

Turning to diving, London Gateway used, and to some extent, pioneered rapid archaeological survey methods that combined acoustic diver tracking, geophysical survey data and integrated real-time digital recording of archaeological observations by divers. Diving proved to be the only means prior to clearance of confirming the type, age, and character of individual sites and of validating, challenging and enhancing the geophysical interpretation. Whilst the in-water conditions meant that it still remained hard for divers to identify and interpret the objects that they were locating on the seabed, the use of acoustic tracking, GIS and the DIVA recording system ensured that the data produced were reliable and transparent.

Although the use of rapid survey methodologies increased and hastened the acquisition of data from non-intrusive diving investigations, the project also recognised and affirmed that intrusive investigations are a necessary component of evaluation underwater. Buried material, which can reasonably be assumed to be 'in context' rather than an intrusion from subsequent deposition or movement, is very important in confidently ascribing age and function to wrecks that otherwise appear on the seabed only as eroded timbers or corroded metalwork. Surface finds, especially in a waterway as heavily used over as many centuries as the Thames, may not provide a sufficiently secure indication. Small excavations or 'sondages' were critical to understanding several of the vessels examined. In view of time constraints and environmental conditions the excavation methods were more robust than might normally be the case on land, or on marine sites whose importance can already be assumed. London Gateway has certainly provided a body of practical experience

upon which discussions about the role and conduct of intrusive investigations in maritime archaeology can build. The project also provides direct examples of the demands of intrusive underwater work in terms of post-excavation planning, resourcing and logistical support.

Perhaps the chief weakness of diving investigations as demonstrated by the project is their cost, which is closely entwined with environmental conditions and uncertainties, and with operational timescales. One limitation of this form of investigation is the short amount of time that could be spent underwater in the tidal Thames, and that all manner of environmental and operational factors could curtail or restrict effective diving. Inevitably, compromises had to be reached in order to find an acceptable balance between affordability and the number and duration of site investigations. As a result the number of sites dived and investigated was limited. Undoubtedly this increased the pressure to be selective in what archaeological tasks might be achieved, and though carefully considered, informed by the AMF, and confirmed by curators it must be acknowledged that decision-making was difficult.

Considering more broadly the role of London Gateway in marine development-led archaeology, it was perhaps inevitable for a ground-breaking project that energy would be expended reworking key points of discussion. Some of this was attributable to the prolonged nature of the development from the EIA process through to the start of dredging, which involved a certain amount of catching-up after periods of quiescence. However, the lack of an existing framework or previously established process contributed to the amount of work required. During this time regulatory and methodological practice was evolving, and serious debate within the project team about what was reasonable and appropriate in this developing environment had to take place. Looking ahead, it is hoped that this volume will ease the path of future projects. Many of the teething problems in developing an overarching strategy to deal with maritime archaeology on a project of this scale have been resolved and this will benefit future port developers, regulators and their advisors. From EIA to depositing archives, it is hoped that lessons learned from London Gateway will help future port developments achieve a workable and sustainable archaeological approach.

Policy and guidance

One difficulty for London Gateway was that there was no directly applicable guidance for the ports industry as to how to deal with the historic environment, or established 'best practice' to emulate. Fortunately, legal frameworks, policies and administrative processes relating to the marine historic environment are now more robust than in the early 2000s. *The Marine and Coastal Access Act* 2009 gives legal effect to the *UK Marine Policy Statement* (HMSO 2011), which includes clear policies on the historic environment that will bind not only the area-based marine plans that will subsequently shape the future licensing of marine works, but also decision-making by all public bodies, including port authorities. New legislation and policy has also been introduced for nationally significant infrastructure projects, including ports that is much clearer about archaeological requirements upon developers (Department for Transport 2012). However, other than outline advice issued by English Heritage (2006), the ports sector is still to develop a corpus of documentation for dealing with the historic environment, in contrast to the marine aggregates and offshore renewable sectors (Wessex Archaeology 2007d; 2010e; 2010f; Oxford Archaeology and George Lambrick 2008; Gribble and Leather 2011). There is still a potential benefit for the development of industry-wide guidance or best-practice to emerge for the ports sector, to facilitate future port development schemes.

Certainty and uncertainty

Although London Gateway made great strides in developing its approach to the uncertainty of what might be present on the seabed and how important it might be, this approach did not progress as far as it might have done. As a consequence, there were still high levels of uncertainty when dredging commenced, and therefore a high risk that one or more important sites might only be found in the course of dredging, which would be both damaging to the archaeological material and disruptive to the dredging programme. All of the additional geophysical data, documentary work and archaeological diving carried out in the course of developing the mitigation proposals were focused on the CMSs and, therefore, on the sites identified as 'Certain', 'Probable' and 'Possible'. The approach to dealing with the far more numerous 'Uncertain' sites remained contentious and, ultimately, the matter was deferred into the dredging programme. Uncertainty arose in two respects: in the area (Yantlet Channel) subject to detailed sidescan survey in 2002, within which there were many anomalies certainly present whose character was uncertain; and in the area beyond the Yantlet, where only low resolution sidescan survey (or no sidescan survey at all) had been undertaken, and where knowledge of what was present on the seabed was very poor. The case for carrying out additional high-resolution sidescan beyond the Yantlet was made within the project team, but not pursued. Exercises to examine in more detail a sample of the 'Uncertains' were mooted, including by additional geophysical and diving investigation, in order to provide a better understanding of what they might actually represent. Such an exercise was not, however, pursued archaeologically. Neither the question of inconsistent sidescan coverage nor the strategy for (not) dealing with the 'Uncertains' was pressed curatorially.

As well as the residual uncertainty associated directly with the scheme, the opportunity to arrive at a satisfactory methodology for addressing uncertainty was also lost, and with it the sort of qualitative and quantitative feedback that could have directly informed future schemes. Specifically, the lack of testing or sampling of the predominantly geophysical anomalies classified as different types of 'Uncertains' meant that it was not possible to develop a better understanding of the relationship between geophysical signatures and their sources on the seabed. Such feedback would have helped resolve some of the uncertainty/risk with respect of the use of geophysics in marine development generally, as well as for London Gateway. The opportunity lost was all the greater because of the extent of the scheme and the number of anomalies it encompassed; although large numbers of anomalies are encountered on large wind farms for example, such schemes are much less intensive in terms of seabed footprint, and the majority of anomalies can be avoided so their character remains unresolved.

The decision not to further investigate the 'Uncertains' prior to dredging led to the acknowledgement in London Gateway's *Protocol for Discoveries during Dredging* that a watching brief would be required around Sea Reach 1 as the quantity of anomalies merited some form of archaeological response. Watching briefs at sea are relatively expensive because of the need to provide archaeological cover for non-stop dredging operations over prolonged periods. Moreover, watching briefs on dredgers are not especially efficient because of the very limited opportunities for archaeologists to observe excavated material, and if something significant is found there will be an even greater cost from disrupting the highly expensive dredging plant. For these reasons, it is better to resort to watching briefs only where there is very specific evidence to suggest that archaeological material will be present; otherwise, it is more cost-effective to resolve as much as possible before dredging commences, and use a finds protocol as a safety net. At London Gateway the preference was to accept a commitment to a watching brief some time later in the process even though it might prove costly and disruptive, rather than bear more immediate costs or face the 'risk' that a site might come to light (even though discovery at an early stage would enable it to be dealt with efficiently).

When approaching the matter of potential wreck sites from the perspective of desk based and geophysical data, it is understandably tempting to focus on what is obvious. Inevitably, this means wreck-like objects. This is especially the case when resources for fieldwork and ground-truthing are limited and doubly so when faced with a mass of data that related to 'Uncertains, Probables and Possibles', when without adequate resourcing to investigate them.

Resources on the project did not allow for sampling of the 'Uncertains, Probables and Possibles' and instead – unsurprisingly – efforts focused on the 'Certains' with a strong bias. Data generated from the percentage of positive 'hits' in each of these categories samples during ground-truthing would have given a good indication of how to interpret different types of geophysical anomalies. Perhaps this approach could have even given a baseline of data for research into how large numbers of anomalies are dealt with in future development work, based on the statistical probability of them being archaeological in nature. Often the more ephemeral anomalies were overlooked, but actually, this is where archaeology of real importance could have been found.

This approach would not be very different to the strategy employed in terrestrial archaeology whereby 'features' on archaeological sites are sampled by percentage. The percentage of sampling is determined by the feature type. For example, the curator might stipulate that 100% of discrete features such as pits will be 'investigated' (in this case fully excavated), 25% of ring-ditches, and 10% of linear features such as boundary ditches. For the marine environment, ground-truthing (sampling) by diving archaeologists would be the most applicable method of investigation. If, for instance, a sample strategy of 100% for the 'Certains', 25% for the 'Probables', 10% for the 'Possibles' and 5% for the 'Uncertains' had been adopted, we would know much more conclusively the potential of the anomaly types.

This sampling approach, at a level appropriate to the wider development and set by the curator, would ensure a balance of mitigation between what is found and what is lost during future development, and would help deliver more accurate archaeological interpretation of geophysical outputs over time. It would also mirror what has come to be accepted practice on terrestrial archaeological sites.

The preference for deferring investigation may have been encouraged by the particular organisational arrangements of London Gateway. Specifically, the PLA was responsible for the pre-clearance and clearance phases in which most archaeological investigation took place, but DP World was responsible for dredging. The question of risk was predominantly a matter for the dredging programme and therefore for DP World rather than the clearance programme of the PLA who were commissioning the investigative works. The interest in resolving uncertainty and reducing risk was not, therefore, distributed evenly. These circumstances may be unusual, but the general point is worth making: it is highly desirable for the development of the mitigation strategy to include the close involvement of the party who will be responsible for mitigation and who will bear its direct and indirect costs. The joining-up of responsibilities can only be helped by fundamental commitment to the goal of good environmental stewardship, as exhibited by the construction team at London Gateway.

Conflict in roles and responsibilities can also arise from the contractual relationship between the developer and its dredging contractor. Whilst the developer carries legal obligations towards the historic environment by virtue of conditions on consent, the developer's ability to give effect to those obligations is highly dependent on practical implementation by the dredging contractor. It is therefore very important that the commercial contract

between the developer and the dredging company has the effect of applying the archaeological conditions on consent to the dredging company. In the absence of a contractual mechanism to give effect to the conditions on consent, the developer can find itself unable – without breaching its contract or invoking expensive variances – to comply with the conditions upon it. This pitfall was avoided in the case of London Gateway by the wholesale incorporation of archaeological documentation into the dredging contract; awareness that archaeological methodologies can acquire a contractually significant role in potentially high-cost decisions about dredging certainly adds a further layer of responsibility to the drafting of documentation such as method statements.

Ultimately, in development-led archaeology, everything comes down to the enforcement of conditions. If the conditions on consent are not sufficiently well worded to be enforced, or no compliance monitoring or enforcement takes place, then the entire process may be undermined. The damage can extend all the way back to the EIA because, as noted above, EIA for major infrastructure schemes incorporates assumptions about subsequent evaluation and mitigation into the initial assessment of impact. That is to say, impacts may be assessed as low or negligible if it is assumed that mitigation will be provided; if the expected mitigation does not occur because compliance is not monitored, then the initial assessment – against which consent was obtained – will prove incorrect. This is not a call for a bureaucratic onslaught, but it is important to underline in a volume about the earlier stages of a project just how close the relationship with the later stages must be. The adequacy of an EIA is only finally apparent when the regulator signs-off compliance with consent. It is therefore important that regulatory expectations are clearly established between all parties and maintained from start to finish. Clear guidance from the regulator as to what is required in terms of archaeological intervention in conjunction with advice from the archaeological advisor as to how this is to be delivered practically based on experience and the understanding of 'best practice', supported by curatorial monitoring of compliance is the best way to remove uncertainty.

Contribution to knowledge

The contribution to the maritime archaeology of the Thames made by London Gateway is concentrated on later vessels. London Gateway has increased awareness of the importance of 20th-century wrecks in particular, such that they have gained greater currency as legitimate concerns for the marine historic environment. Later 19th- and 20th-century wrecks have become problematic for archaeologists as a result of development-led projects for ports like London Gateway, but also for marine aggregates, cables and pipelines, and offshore wind farms. Prior to the emergence of marine development-led archaeology in the UK in the mid–late 1990s, there had been very little expressly archaeological work on metal-hulled wrecks in the UK, with the exception of wrecks such as the *Iona II* and submarine wrecks like *Resurgam*. The development of relatively high-resolution multibeam – which is especially suited to imaging metal wrecks – was also providing new means to investigate more recent wrecks, but interest was technical (in terms of methods) or social/historical rather than archaeological. Recent wrecks are, however, the most commonly encountered in development-led archaeology and require a cogent response in terms of investigative methodologies and frameworks for assessing importance and impact. London Gateway directly provided a testing ground for archaeological approaches to later wrecks; but it also informed and inspired initiatives occurring elsewhere, especially through the Aggregate Levy Sustainability Fund (ALSF) which saw significant strategic funding going to projects concerned with metal wrecks (Hamel 2011). In turn, such projects have informed the development of curatorial guidance on wrecks of exactly the sort that was so desperately needed in the earlier phases of London Gateway (English Heritage 2012a; 2012b).

The project has been relatively successful in terms of identifying the wrecks of small vessels and boats, an under-represented category of wreck in both local and national inventories. The project has established the potential of such wrecks to comprise and contain remains of structure, equipment, cargo and possessions that – even if of recent date – have the potential to inform and increase the awareness of maritime life in and around the estuary. Arguably this potential has yet to be fully realised, in that only very limited time was spent investigating such sites, and the archaeological methods – pressed by time and environment – could not be as painstaking as have been employed on older and grander vessels in UK waters.

Equally, because they were to be safeguarded *in situ*, only very limited investigations were carried out on the two sites associated with the *London*, but they have nonetheless helped place the understanding of this wreck on a firmer base, to confirm its importance and to safeguard it from dredging. The 'Iron Bar Wreck', whose significance is not yet clear, has similarly been secured from impacts from the scheme.

Although limited, the London Gateway investigations have repeatedly demonstrated that significant archaeological material survives beneath the Thames, including good survival of ship structure and organic artefacts. Such survival has occurred despite previous clearance and dredging, and the generally hostile environment. In this, London Gateway has demonstrated the fallacy of presuming that previous undersea work will have removed all traces of the past; both on individual sites and across extensive areas, the actual presence of archaeological material can only be established on the basis of evidence from the seabed, not by recollections or assumptions.

As noted previously, London Gateway is an extensive project and – by the time dredging is complete – it will have substantially modified the seabed and the archaeological record that it contained. Despite its physical extents, London Gateway still only scratches the surface of the potential maritime archaeology of the Thames. The newly dredged channel is still relatively narrow compared to the breadth of the Thames, even in the upper reaches of the Yantlet. In the outer estuary, only a tiny fraction of the seabed has been comprehensively investigated. Admittedly, dredging has concentrated on the main channel, which is likely to have seen a concentration of larger, deeper draught ships powered by steam or internal combustion engines. But maritime use of the estuary has not been so constrained, especially in earlier periods. Smaller vessels have greater freedom with respect to water depth and sailing vessels must make broader use of maritime space to harness the wind, and even the record of bigger metal ships shows that they are widely distributed. Overall then, the Thames can be expected to hold very many more sites of archaeological interest than have been affected by this scheme.

Conclusion

To conclude, London Gateway has provided key lessons that have already been absorbed by other major infrastructure projects, such as the importance of early and thorough integration of geophysical survey and interpretation with desk- and field-based approaches. London Gateway has demonstrated that site avoidance, redesign and minor realignment should be considered from the earliest stage and that they should continue to remain available as mitigation options, because intrusive mitigation will often be expensive and operationally difficult to achieve. A joined-up approach to EIA/consent, design-phase investigations and construction is also highly desirable, so that the costs and benefits of actions to reduce uncertainty are considered in the overall context of a finished scheme, not just in terms of what might be deferred past the current stage. Historic environment issues should certainly not be ignored, especially as thresholds of awareness, expectation and requirement have – as noted above – risen in association with the introduction of the *Marine and Coastal Access Act* 2009 and associated policy. A corresponding increase in engagement by curators and regulators can be anticipated, and this is to be welcomed where it increases certainty amongst all the parties involved. In the absence of certainty, archaeologists engaged in development-led archaeology can appear as unwelcome messengers rather than integral members of the development team. Archaeology can be a complicated matter for major marine developments, requiring close collaboration and problem-solving; as numerous examples show, solutions flow more swiftly where there is openness and trust.

Figure 55: Aerial view of London Gateway port site

Looking ahead, archaeologists are becoming more certain about questions of significance – including the importance of 20th-century wrecks – due to the emergence of frameworks and guidance about site importance/significance emerging from a range of projects and initiatives (eg Wessex Archaeology 2006a; English Heritage 2012a; 2012b). Uncertainty about the archaeological character of seabed anomalies and features may also decrease due to improvements in geophysical technology, especially in resolution, which makes it easier to 'see' anomalies more clearly. The processing and interpretation of large geophysical datasets has become more effective and streamlined as a result of dealing with very large areas of seabed for offshore wind farms in particular. Diver-based survey methodologies are also improving, through the combination of underwater positioning and scanning technologies, so that there is scope to achieve more and better recording within the limited time available.

Whilst major steps are being taken towards reducing uncertainty and better understanding site importance,

both are likely to remain sources of complexity. Technologies are improving, increasing the amount of data that field-investigation can return as well as the scope for more complex processing, interpretation and display. But the cost of deploying geophysical equipment, archaeological divers, ROVs and so on is likely to remain high, as is the cost of increasingly sophisticated processing and manipulation. As a result, pressure will be maintained on strategies for investigation and mitigation, and on the level of assessment and interpretation that is sufficient or advisable. The task of achieving major marine development that is sustainable with respect to the historic environment will continue to be demanding, but it is hoped that knowledge of the experience of London Gateway will make it at least a little easier. Of course the sea will carry on being a temperamental environment, with currents, weather and visibility all seeming to conspire to constrain the efforts of archaeologists. But if its history had been benign, the Thames would be much less interesting today.

Site ID	Name	Archaeological interest at EIA (Mitigation group)	Desk based research	Marine Geophysics			Diving		Mitigation			Clearance without further mitigation
				Sidescan sonar	Multibeam bathymetry	Magnet-ometer	Stage I	Stage II	Avoidance	Recording and recovery	Resettlement	
5005	*Letchworth*	Possible	✓	✓	✓		✓		✓			
5008	*Argus*	Possible	✓	✓	✓				✓			
5010/5012	*Dovenby*	Probable	✓	✓	✓	✓	✓			✓		
5011	*Atherton*	Possible	✓	✓	✓				✓			
5013	HMT *Ash*	Possible	✓	✓	✓							✓
5019	*London* ('King')	Certain	✓	✓	✓	✓	✓	✓	✓			
5020	'Iron Bar' wreck	Probable	✓	✓			✓		✓			
5029	*London*	Certain	✓		✓		✓	✓	✓			
5041	Unknown Aircraft	Possible	✓	✓	✓	✓						✓
5046	Wreck NW of Sea Reach 1	Probable	✓	✓		✓	✓	✓		✓		
5050	Aircraft/Coal dump	Probable	✓	✓	✓	✓	✓					✓
5051	Mid-Blyth Wreck	Probable	✓	✓	✓	✓	✓	✓		✓		
5056	East Oaze Light Vessel	Probable	✓	✓			✓				✓	✓
5057	*Aisha*	Possible	✓	✓	✓							✓
5063	HMT *Amethyst*	Possible	✓	✓	✓				✓			
5070	MV *Ryal*	Possible	✓	✓	✓				✓		✓	
5100	*Dynamo*	Possible	✓	✓	✓				✓			
5124	Unknown	Probable	✓	✓	✓		✓					✓
5185	'Ancient Wreck'	Probable	✓	✓	✓	✓	✓					✓
5195	Anti-submarine Boom	Possible	✓	✓	✓	✓	✓		✓	✓		
5204	'Pottery Wreck'	Certain	✓	✓	✓		✓	✓		✓		
5230	Brick Barge	Probable	✓	✓	✓	✓	✓	✓		✓		
5960	*Storm*	Possible	✓	✓	✓							✓
5961	*Erna Boldt*	Possible	✓	✓	✓							✓
6595	Halcrow A5 ★	Probable	✓	✓								✓
7345	Unknown Wreck	Uncertain	✓	✓	✓		✓					✓
7404	Natural/Buried (60m feature)	Probable	✓	✓	✓	✓	✓			✓		✓
7543	German Aircraft	Probable	✓	✓	✓	✓	✓	✓				
7563	Natural/Buried feature	Probable	✓	✓	✓	✓	✓					✓

★ Site is now considered to have been highlighted by Halcrow as a result of a positioning error

Appendix: Table A1: A summary of all sites (all sites have Clearance Mitigation Statements (CMSs)

80

London Gateway. Maritime Archaeology in the Thames Estuary

Bibliography

Primary sources:

ADM 53/101095 Admiralty: and Ministry of Defence: Navy Department: *Ships' Logs, Amethyst, 1938 Sept 26–Oct 13*, National Archives, Kew

TNA ADM 53/94739 Admiralty: and Ministry of Defence: Navy Department: *Ships' Logs, Amethyst, 1936 Feb 20–Mar 24*, National Archives, Kew

TNA ADM 1/9936

TNA ADM 1/11295, Admiralty and Ministry of Defence Navy Department: Correspondence and Papers: SERIES I: 1938–1945 (plus strays 1892–1937): BOARDS OF INQUIRY AND DISCIPLINARY COURTS (Code 29), *Loss of HM trawler ASH by mining: board of enquiry*, 1941, National Archives, Kew

TNA ADM 1/11651, Admiralty and Ministry of Defence Navy Department: Correspondence and Papers: SERIES I: 1938–1945 (plus strays 1892–1937): HONOURS AND AWARDS (Code 85), *Awards to personnel of H.M. Ships ASH, ACACIA, BAY, DEODOR and WALNUT for good services in Channel convoys*, 1941, National Archives, Kew

TNA ADM 267/113, Admiralty: Department of the Director of Naval Construction: later Director General Ships: Damage Reports and Files: Shell and bomb, SS *Letchworth*, 1939–1944 The National Archives, Kew

TNA ADM 1/18128

DD/655/21, Doulton & Watts' price list of 1873, Hammersmith and Fulham Archives

Lloyd's List, London

Lloyd's Register of British and Foreign Shipping, London

Lloyd's of London, 1920–1994 *Lloyd's Weekly Casualty Reports*, London

Mercurius Politicus, no.320, 31 July 1656

NMR TQ 98 SW 166, Monument No. 1401527, Junkers Ju87B-1 (5227) 6G+KS at the entrance to the Thames Estuary, National Monuments Record, Swindon

NMR TQ 98 SE 131, Monument No. 1400382, 20th Century Boom at Pig's Bay, National Monuments Record, Swindon

Secondary sources:

Adams, J, Holk, A F L, Maarleveld, Th, J, and Volksgezondheid en Cultur. Afdeling Achaeologie Onder water Netherlands. Ministerie van Welzijn, 1990 *Dredgers and archaeology: ship finds from the Slufter*, Alphen aan den Rijn: Afdeling Archaeologie Onder water, Ministerie van Welzijn, Volksgezheid en Cultuur

Allen, M J, and Gardiner, J P, 2000 *Our Changing Coast: a survey of the intertidal archaeology of Langstone Harbour, Hampshire*, CBA Res Rep **124**, London

Auer, J, and Firth, A, 2007 The 'Gresham Ship': an interim report on a 16th-century wreck from Princes Channel, Thames Estuary, *Post-medieval Archaeol* **41** (**2**), 222–41

Biddle, M, and Webster, J, 2005 Green glass bottles, in M Biddle, *Nonsuch Palace: the material culture of a noble Restoration household*, 266–301, Oxford, Oxbow Books

Biddulph, E, 2010 *Time and Tide: the archaeology of Stanford Wharf Nature Reserve*, Oxford Archaeology/DP World/Thames Gateway

Biddulph, E, Foreman, S, Stafford, E, Stansbie, D, and Nicholson, R, 2012 *London Gateway Iron Age and Roman salt making in the Thames Estuary: excavation at Stanford Wharf Nature Reserve, Essex*, Oxford Archaeol Monogr **18**, Oxford

Blackmore, H L, 1976 *The Armouries of the Tower of London. I Ordnance*, DoE, London

Booth, P, Champion, C, Foreman, S, Garwood, P, Glass, H, Munby, J, and Reynolds, A, 2011 *On Track: the archaeology of High Speed 1 Section 1 in Kent*, Oxford Wessex Archaeol Monogr **4**, Oxford

Boston, C, Witkin A, Boyle A, and Wilkinson D R P, 2008 *Safe Moor'd in Greenwich Tier: a study of the skeletons of Royal Navy sailors and marines excavated at the Royal Naval Hospital Greenwich*, Oxford Archaeol Monogr **5**, Oxford

Bradley, R, Haselgrove, C, Vander Linden, M, and Webley, L, 2011 *Development-led Archaeology in Northeast Europe*, Oxbow Books, Oxford

Brandon, P, and Short, B, 1990 *The South East from AD 1000*, Longman, London

Bryn, P, Jasinski, M E, and Søreide, F, 2007 *Ormen Lange?: pipelines and shipwrecks*, Universitetsforlaget, Oslo

Campbell, G, 1974 *China Tea Clippers*, Adlard Coles, London

Castro, F, 2005 Arade River Archaeological Complex: Dredges and Archaeology, *Int J Naut Archaeol* **34.1**, 51–61

Cocker, M P, 1993 *Mine Warfare Vessels of the Royal Navy, 1908 to Date*, Airlife Publishing, Shrewsbury

Colledge, J J, 1989 *Ships of the Royal Navy*, Greenhill Books, London

Curryer, B N, 1999 *Anchors: an illustrated history*, Chatham Publishing, London

Davies, J D, 2008 *Pepys's Navy: ships, men and warfare 1649–1689*, Seaforth Publishing, Barnsley

Davis, R, 1962 *The rise of the English shipping industry in the seventeenth and eighteenth centuries*, Macmillan, London

Dawkes, G, Goodburn, D, and Rogers, P W, 2009 Lightening the load: five 19th-century river lighters at Erith on the River Thames, UK, *Int J Naut Archaeol* **38**(1), 71–89

Department of the Environment, 1990 *Planning Policy Guidance: archaeology and planning* (PPG 16), HMSO, London

Department for Transport, 2012 *National Policy Statement for Ports*, HMSO, London

de la Bédoyère, G, 2000 *Battles over Britain: the archaeology of the air war*, Tempus, Stroud

English Heritage, 2006 *Ports: the impact of development on the maritime historic environment*, English Heritage online publication: http://www.helm.org.uk/upload/pdf/Ports-policy.pdf

English Heritage, 2010 *Accessing England's Protected Wreck Sites: guidance notes for divers and archaeologists*, English Heritage online publication: http://www.english-heritage.org.uk/publications/guidance-for-divers/

English Heritage, 2012 *National Planning Policy Framework*, English Heritage, London

English Heritage, 2012a *Ships and Boats: Prehistory to 1840 Introductions to Heritage Assets*, English Heritage, London

English Heritage 2012b *Ships and Boats: Prehistory to Present. Designation Selection Guide*, English Heritage

Essex County Council, 2010 *The Greater Thames Estuary Historic Environment Research Framework*. Essex County Council/English Heritage online publication: http://www.english-heritage.org.uk/content/publications/publicationsNew/greater-thames-estuary-res-framework-2010/gt-research-framework-2010-pt1.pdf

Firth, A J, 2011 Submerged prehistory in the North Sea, in A Catsambis, B Ford and D Hamilton (eds), *The Oxford Handbook of Maritime Archaeology*, 786–808, Oxford University Press, New York

Flatman, J, and Doeser, J, 2010 The international management of marine aggregates and its relation to maritime archaeology, *The Historic Environment* **1**(2), 160–84

FLOAT, 2010 Fleetwood Online Archive of Trawlers, record no. 689, http://float-trawlers.lancashire.gov.uk

Fox, F, 1980 *Great Ships: the battlefleet of King Charles II*, Conway Maritime Press, London

Fox, F L, 2012 The London of 1656: her history and armament, *Trans Naval Dockyards Soc* **8**, 57–76

Framework Archaeology, 2010 *Landscape Evolution in the Middle Thames Valley: Heathrow Terminal 5 Excavations Vol. 2*. Oxford/Salisbury, Framework Archaeol Monogr **3**

Gawronski, J, Kist, B, and Stockvis-Boetzelear, O, (eds), 1992 *Hollandia Compendium*: acontribution to the history, archaeology, classification and lexography of a 150 ft Dutch East Indiaman (1740–1750), Elsevier, Amsterdam

Gilman, P, 1997 Fortifications, in Glazebrook (1997), 67–9

Glazebrook, J (ed.), *Research and Archaeology: a framework for the Eastern Counties, 1. Resource Assessment*, East Anglian Archaeol Occ Paper **3**, Norwich

Goodburn, D, Meddens, F, Holden, S, and Phillpotts, C, 2011 Linking land and navy: archaeological investigations at the site of the Woolwich Royal Dockyard, south-eastern England, *Int J Naut Archaeol* **40**(2), 306–27

Gould, S, 1997 *The archaeology of industrialisation and manufacture 1750–1960*, in Glazebrook (1997), 73–9

Gravesham Borough Council, 2007 *Facts on Gravesend: Henry VIII's Blockhouse*, Gravesham Borough Council

Gribble, J, and Leather, S, 2011 Offshore geotechnical investigations and historic environmental analysis: guidance for the renewable energy sector, Emu Ltd report for COWRIE Ltd, ref GEOARCH-09

Gundersen, J, 2010 Archaeological Challenges in Cooperating on a Large-Scale Construction Project: The Immersed Tunnel, Oslo, Norway, *The Historic Environment* 1 (1) (June 1), 6–26. doi:10.1179/175675010X12662480109072

Hamel, A, 2011 *Wrecks on the Seabed*, MALSF Science Monogr **6**, http://www.cefas.defra.gov.uk/media/463755/monograph6-web.pdf

Harrower, J, 1998 *Wilson Line: the history and fleet of Thos. Wilson, Sons Co. and Ellerman's Wilson Line Ltd.*, World Ship Society, Gravesend

Hewitt, N, 2008 *Coastal Convoys 1939–1945: the indestructible highway*, Pen & Sword Maritime, Barnsley

Hirschel, E, Prem, H, and Madelung, G, 2001 *Aeronautical Research in Germany: from Lilienthal until today*, Bernard & Graefe Verlag, Bonn

HMSO, 1947 *Ships of the Royal Navy: statement of losses during the Second World War*, London

HMSO, 2011 *UK Maritime Policy Statement*, London

Hurst, J G, Neal, D S, and Beuningen, H J E van, 1986 *Pottery Produced and Traded in North-West Europe 1350–1650*, Rotterdam Papers **6**, Rotterdam

Jackson, G, 1983 *The History and Archaeology of Ports*, World's Work Ltd, Surrey

Johns, C, Camidge, K, and Northover, P, 2011 *Wreck of the Barque Antoinette, Camel Estuary, Padstow, Cornwall*, Cornwall Council Historic Environment Service, Truro

Kay, A, 2004 *Junkers Aircraft & Engines 1913–1945*, Putnam Aeronautical Books, London

Larn, R, and Larn, B, 1996 *Shipwreck Index of the British Isles, Volume 3: The South Coast*. Lloyds Register of Shipping, London

Lavery, B, 2006 *Churchill's Navy: the ships, men and organisation*, 1939–1945, Conway Maritime, London

Layman, R D, 2002 *Naval Aviation in the First World War: its impact and influence*, Caxton Editions, London

Lund, P, and Ludlam, H, 1971 *Trawlers Go to War: the story of "Harry Tate's Navy"*, Foulsham & Co, London

Maarleveld, Th, J, 1989 Marine archaeology and the planning of large-scale sand-extraction: an example from the Netherlands, in G Trotzig and G Vahlne (eds), *Archaeology and Society: Large Scale Rescue Operations – Their Possibilities and Problems*, 247–55, ICAHM Rep **1**, Stockholm

MacRae, J A, and Waine, C V, 1990 *The Steam Collier Fleets*, Waine Research Publications, Albrighton

Marsden, P, 1996 *Ships of the Port of London: twelfth to seventeenth centuries AD*, London, English Heritage Archaeol Rep **5**

Martin, C J M, 1995 The Cromwellian shipwreck off Duart Point, Mull: an interim report, *Int J Naut Archaeol* **24**(1), 15–32

McCarthy, M (ed.), 2010 *Iron, Steel and Steamship Archaeology: proceedings of the 2nd Australian seminar, held at Perth, Melbourne and Sydney, 2006*, ANCEMA, Freemantle

Meade, R W, 1869 *A Treatise on Naval Architecture and Ship-building or An Exposition of the Elementary Principles involved in the Science and Practice of Naval* Construction, J B Lippincott, Philadelphia

Merritt, O, Parham, D, and McElvogue, D, 2007 *Enhancing Our Understanding of the Marine Historic Environment: navigational hazards project final report*, Bournemouth University, Bournemouth

Middlemiss, N L, 1995 *British Shipbuilding Yards 3: Belfast, Merseyside, Barrow and all other area*, Shield Publications, Newcastle-Upon-Tyne

Milne, G, McKewan, C, and Goodburn, D, 1998 *Nautical Archaeology on the Foreshore: hulk recording on the Medway*, Royal Commission on Historic Monuments England, Swindon

Morison, S E, 1975 *History of United States Naval Operations in World War II, Volume I. The Battle of the Atlantic 1939–1943*, Little, Brown & Company, New York

Murphy, P, 2009 *The English Coast: a history and a prospect*, Continuum, London

Nayling, N, 1998 *The Magor Pill Medieval Wreck*, CBA Res Rep **115**, York

Nayling, N, 2005a *London Gateway Project: Yantlet Channel Diving Inspection Report 1*, unpubl rep

Nayling, N, 2005b *London Gateway Project: Yantlet Channel Diving Inspection Report 2*, unpubl rep

Oxford Archaeology, and Lambrick, G, 2008 *Guidance for Assessment of Cumulative Impacts on the Historic Environment from Offshore Renewable Energy*, COWRIE project reference CIARCH-11-2006, COWRIE Ltd

Pedersen, L, Fischer, A, Aaby, B, and Storebæltsforbindelsen, A/S, 1997 *The Danish Storebælt since the Ice Age?: man, sea and forest*, A/S Storebælt Fixed Link in co-operation with Kalundborg Regional Museum, Danish National Forest & Nature Agency (the Ministry of Environment and Energy), Copenhagen

Port of London Authority, 2005a Internal Rep 342/79

Port of London Authority, 2005b Internal Rep 341/19

Port of London Authority, 2005c Internal Rep 343/01

Port of London Authority, 2005d Internal Rep 343/02

Port of London Authority, 2005e Internal Rep 343/26

Port of London Authority, 2005f Internal Rep 343/93

Port of London Authority, 2005g Internal Rep 343/99

Port of London Authority, 2005h Internal Rep 343/11

Port of London Authority, 2005i Internal Rep 201/45

Powell A B, Booth, P, Crockett, A D, and Fitzpatrick, A P, 2008 *The Archaeology of the M6 Toll 2000–2002*. Oxford/Salisbury, Oxford Wessex Archaeology Monogr **2**

Redknap, M, 1990 The Albion and Hindostan: the fate of two outward-bound East Indiaman, *Int J Naut Archaeol* **19**(1), 23–30

Rodger, N A M, 1997 *The Safeguard of the Sea: a naval history of Britain I: 660–1649*, Harper Collins, London

Rodger, N A M, 2007 *Command of the Ocean: a naval history of Britain, 1649–1815*, Penguin Books, London

Royal, J G and McManamon, J M, 2010 At the Transition from Late Medieval to Early Modern: the Archaeology of Three Wrecks from Turkey, *Int J Naut Archaeol* **39**(2), 327–344

Satchell, J, 2012, *Maritime Archives and The Crown Estate: Project Report*, Hampshire and Wight Trust for Maritime Archaeology, Southampton

Simper, R, 1982 *Britain's Maritime Heritage*, David & Charles, Newton Abbot

Simper, R, 1997 The Wash and Thames Estuary, in J Mannering and B Greenhill (eds), *The Chatham Directory of Inshore Craft: traditional working vessels of the British Isles*, Chatham Publishing, London, 60–100

Slaven, A, 1992 *British Shipbuilding 1500–2010: a history*, Crucible Books, Lancaster

Starkey, D (ed.), 1999 *Shipping Movements in the Ports of the United Kingdom 1871–1913: a statistical profile*, University of Exeter Press, Exeter

Stahl, J, 1995 *Neptunwerft: 1. Band der Schriften des Rostocker* Schiffahrtsmuseums, Redieck and Schade GbR, Rostock

Sturt, F, and Dix, J K, 2009 *Outer Thames Estuary Regional Environmental Characterisation*, ALSF/MEPF (DEFRA), EMU Ltd, London

Talbot-Booth, E C, 1940 *Merchant Ships*, Marston & Co, London

Thomas, P N, 1992 *British Ocean Tramps Volume 1. Builders & Cargoes*, Waine Research Publications, Albrighton

Toghill, G, 2003 *Royal Navy Trawlers 1: Admiralty vessels*, Maritime Books, Liskeard

Timby, J, Brown, R, Biddulph, E, Hardy, A, and Powell, AB, 2007A *Slice of Rural Essex: archaeological discoveries from the A120 between Stansted Airport and Braintree*, Oxford/Salisbury, Oxford Wessex Archaeol Monogr **1**

Van Tilburg, H K, 1994 Zero-visibility diving on the *Maple Leaf*: the tricks of the trade, *Int J Naut Archaeol* **23**(4), 315–318

Ville, S, 1993 The wooden sailing ship: over 300 tons, in R Gardiner (ed.), *Sail's Last Century: the merchant sailing ships 1830–1930*, 20–41, Conway Maritime Press, London

Waine, C V, and Fenton, RS, 1994 *Steam Coasters and Short Sea Traders*, Waine Research Publications, Albrighton

Ward, J, 2004 *Hitler's Stuka Squadrons: the Ju 87 at war, 1936–1945*, The History Press Ltd, Stroud

Weal, J, 2000 *Ju 88 Kampfgeschwader on the Western Front*, Osprey, Oxford

Wessex Archaeology, 2004 *Wrecks on the Seabed. Assessment, Evaluation and Recording, Year 2* Report, unpubl rep 51536.04

Wessex Archaeology, 2006a *On the Importance of Shipwrecks: Vols 1–2*, Wessex Archaeology, unpubl rep 58591.02a–b

Wessex Archaeology, 2006b *Swash Channel, Poole harbour Approach, Dorset. Designated Site Assessment Archaeological report*, web-published rep ref 53111.03gg

Wessex Archaeology, 2006c *West Bay, Dorset. Undesignated Site Assessment: Full Report*, unpubl rep 53111.02k–7b

Wessex Archaeology, 2006d *Diamond, Sarn Badrig. Designated Site Assessment: Full Report*, unpubl rep 53111.03u

Wessex Archaeology, 2007a *London Gateway Clearance Programme. Diving First Tranche. Field Report. 66892.5230. Unknown (Brick Barge)*, unpubl rep

Wessex Archaeology, 2007b *London Gateway Clearance Programme. Diving First Tranche. Field Report. 66892.7345. Unknown*, unpubl rep

Wessex Archaeology, 2007c *London Gateway Clearance Programme. Diving First Tranche. Field Report. 66892.5012. Dovenby North*, unpubl rep

Wessex Archaeology 2007d *Historic Environment Guidance for the Offshore Renewable Energy Sector*, prepared for COWRIE Ltd

Wessex Archaeology, 2008a *Aircraft Crash Sites at Sea: a scoping study*, web-published rep ref 66641.02

Wessex Archaeology, 2008b *Archaeological Diving Investigation 'The King'*, unpubl rep 66892.02

Wessex Archaeology, 2008c *London Gateway Port: Channel Clearance and Dredging. In-water Archaeological Observation and Recording, Final Report. Wreck 5051 (Unknown)*, unpubl rep 66896.5051.01

Wessex Archaeology, 2008d *London Gateway Port: Channel Clearance and Dredging. In-water Archaeological Observation and Recording, Final Report. Wreck 5204 (Pottery Wreck)*, unpubl rep 66896.5204.01

Wessex Archaeology, 2008e *London Gateway Clearance Programme. Anti Submarine Boom Further Documentary Research. Technical Report*, unpubl rep 66893.01

Wessex Archaeology, 2009a *The Maritime Archaeology of the Welsh Slate Trade*, unpubl rep 53111.02s–4

Wessex Archaeology, 2009b *The Maritime Archaeology of the Welsh Coal Trade*, unpubl rep 53111.02s–3

Wessex Archaeology 2010a *East of England Designated Wrecks Marine Geophysical Survey and Interpretation*, upubl rep ref 71770.02

Wessex Archaeology, 2010b *Wrecks off the coast of Wales: Marine geophysical surveys and interpretation*, unpubl rep 53111.02s–5

Wessex Archaeology, 2010c TEDA *Marine Aggregate Regional Environmental Assessment. Technical Report: Archaeology*, unpubl rep

Wessex Archaeology, 2010d *London Gateway: a maritime history*, Salisbury

Wessex Archaeology, 2010e *Protocol for Archaeological Discoveries: offshore renewables projects*, Wessex Archaeology/Crown Estate web published report: http://www.thecrownestate.co.uk/media/122838/pad_offshore_renewables.pdf

Wessex Archaeology, 2010f *Model Clauses for Archaeological Written Schemes of Investigation: offshore renewables projects*. Wessex Archaeology/Crown Estate web published report: http://www.thecrownestate.co.uk/media/122834/wsi_renewables.pdf

Wessex Archaeology, 2011a *Assessing Boats and Ships 1860–1913: archaeological desk-based assessment*, unpubl rep ref 70861.1

Wessex Archaeology, 2011b *Assessing Boats and Ships 1914–1938*, unpubl rep ref 70861.2

Wessex Archaeology, 2011c *Assessing Boats and Ships 1939–1950, archaeological desk-based assessment*, unpubl rep ref 70861.3

Wessex Archaeology, 2011d *Assessing Boats and Ships 1860–1950: methodology report*, unpubl rep ref 70861.4

Wessex Archaeology, 2011e *The Approaches to Bristol and its Historic Anchorages*, unpubl rep ref 76621.01

Wessex Archaeology, 2011f *The London, Southend, Thames Estuary. Designated Site Assessment: Archaeological Report*, unpubl rep 53111.03xxx

Wessex Archaeology, 2012a *The London, Southend, Thames Estuary. Designated Site Assessment: Archaeological Report*, unpubl rep 53111.03zzz

Wessex Archaeology 2012b GAD 23 *(the Bowsprit Wreck), Goodwin Sands, Kent*, unpubl rep 53111.02k–25

Wessex Archaeology, forthcoming *The Hindostan, off Margate, Thames Estuary. Undesignated Site Assessment*, unpubl rep

Winchester, J, 2005 *Aircraft of World War II*, Thunder Bay Press

Williams, J, and Brown, N (eds), 1999 *An Archaeological Research Framework for the Greater Thames Estuary*, Essex County Council, Chelmsford

Wragg, E, 2010a *Wreck Site 343/26 5046 Northwest of Sea Reach 1 Thames Estuary: an archaeological assessment report*, unpubl rep, Thames Discovery Programme

Wragg, E, 2010b *Artefacts Removed From Wreck Site 343/26 5046, Northwest of Sea Reach 1, Thames Estuary*, unpubl rep code SRE 10, Thames Discovery Programme

Wragg, E, 2010c *Wreck Site 341/02 5051 'Unknown (Old Timbers and Concrete)', Mid Blyth, Thames Estuary*, unpubl rep code MBE 10, Thames Discovery Programme

Wragg, E, 2010d *Wreck Site 343/99 5230 'Unknown (Brick Barge)': an archaeological assessment report*, unpubl rep, Thames Discovery Programme

Woodman, R, 2005 *Keepers of the Sea: the story of the Trinity House Yachts and Tenders* Chaffcutter Books, Ware

Young, J M, 1989 *Britain's Sea War: a diary of ship losses, 1939–1945*, Stephens, Wellingborough

Websites

Maritime Journal: http://www.maritimejournal.com/news 101/uk_government_rejects_dibden_bay_proposal (Information No. 19326)

Index

by Susan M. Vaughan